Material
Offerings and
the Lord's
Move Today

The Holy Word for Morning Revival

Watchman Nee
Witness Lee

Living Stream Ministry
Anaheim, California

First Edition, March 1999.

ISBN 978-0-7363-0531-0

Published by

Living Stream Ministry
2431 W. La Palma Ave., Anaheim, CA 92801 U.S.A.
P. O. Box 2121, Anaheim, CA 92814 U.S.A.

Printed in the United States of America

14 15 16 17 18 14 / 10 9 8 7 6 5

Contents

Week	Title	Page
	Preface	v

MATERIAL OFFERINGS
AND THE LORD'S MOVE TODAY

Week	Title	Page
	General Subject	1
1	Principles of Material Offerings (1)	
	Day 1	2
2	Principles of Material Offerings (2)	
	Day 1	16
3	Material Offerings and Full-time Service	
	Day 1	30
4	Material Offerings for the Lord's Move	
	Day 1	44
5	Principles of Material Offerings (3)	
	Day 1	58
	Recovery Version Reading Schedule	72
	Daily Verse Cards	77

Preface

1. This book is intended as an aid to believers in developing a daily time of morning revival with the Lord in His word. At the same time, it provides a review of crucial extracts from the ministry concerning material offerings and the Lord's move today. Through intimate contact with the Lord in His word, the believers can be constituted with life and truth and thereby equipped to prophesy in the meetings of the church unto the building up of the Body of Christ.

2. The content of this book is taken primarily from the text and footnotes of the Recovery Version of the Bible, selections from the writings of Watchman Nee and Witness Lee, and *Hymns,* all of which are published by Living Stream Ministry.

3. The book is divided into weeks. Each week presents six daily portions, a hymn, and then some space for writing. Each daily portion covers one main point and begins with a section entitled "Morning Nourishment." This section contains selected verses that can provide rich spiritual nourishment through intimate fellowship with the Lord. The "Morning Nourishment" is followed by a section entitled "Today's Reading," a portion of ministry related to the day's main point. Each day's portion concludes with a short list of references for further reading and some space for the saints to make notes concerning their spiritual inspiration, enlightenment, and enjoyment to serve as a reminder of what they have received of the Lord that day.

4. The space provided at the end of each week is for composing a short prophecy. This prophecy can be composed by considering all our daily notes, the "harvest" of our inspirations during the week, and preparing a main point with some sub-points to be spoken in the church meetings for the organic building up of the Body of Christ.

5. The footnotes and references in the Recovery Version of the Bible were written by Witness Lee. All of the other

works cited in this publication, unless otherwise noted, were written by Watchman Nee and Witness Lee.

General Subject:

MATERIAL OFFERINGS
AND THE LORD'S MOVE TODAY

Morning Nourishment

1 Thes. For they themselves report concerning us what
1:9   kind of entrance we had toward you and how you
      turned to God from the idols to serve a living and
      true God.
Matt. Blessed are the poor in spirit, for theirs is the king-
5:3   dom of the heavens.

Today's Reading

The five points [below] concern a Christian's attitude towards money, as seen in the New Testament. This is our way of dealing with mammon. We have to deal with mammon in an absolute way. Today a Christian should begin his pathway of revival from his experience of deliverance from mammon. We have to be delivered from mammon.

First, the Bible describes mammon as an idol. The Bible always places mammon in opposition to God. There is no true atheist in this world. The Bible does not recognize non-Christians as adherents of other religions. It classifies men into only two categories: those who are serving God and those who are serving mammon. Other religions, such as Buddhism, Mohammedanism, Taoism, etc., are counterfeit religions. There are only two true objects of worship: mammon and God. Therefore, mammon is an idol; it is an object apart from God that is being worshipped. It is unthinkable for a Christian to pray and read the Bible on the one hand, and bow to Kuanyin (a Buddhist goddess) and burn incense to her on the other hand. The minimum requirement of being a Christian is to turn from idols to serve the living God (1 Thes. 1:9). We all agree that we have to cast down all idols. Yet we do not consider mammon to be an evil thing. This is a gross mistake. We must be clear that we cannot worship idols, and we must equally be clear that we cannot worship mammon. We cannot serve God and mammon. Mammon is an idol.

We must never tell others that they need to offer their

mammon because we need to build meeting halls or because we need to take care of the work or the poor. We should never lower the meaning of consecration to the level of satisfying needs. This denigrates the meaning of consecration. We deal with mammon not because of our need but because it is an idol. A man can say that he does not want to offer money for building meeting halls. He also can say that he does not want to care for the poor brothers and sisters, but he must not worship idols. Dealing with mammon is not a matter of being rich or poor; it is a matter of idolatry....We have to see that mammon is diametrically opposed to God. We should not tell others to give up mammon because we are short of money. If this were the case, they might conclude that they can worship mammon when there is not a lack of money. We must rid ourselves of mammon because mammon is God's enemy. It is terribly wrong for a Christian to remain in a temple of Dagon. It is equally wrong for the idol of mammon to remain in the saints' homes. We are not speaking about being rich or poor. We are saying that mammon as an idol must be removed.

We have to show Christians that mammon is an idol; it is something that demands worship. It is something apart from God. This problem must be addressed. The Bible does not say that all those who are poor are blessed; it says that those who are poor in spirit are blessed. Being poor in spirit is being poor voluntarily. All the beggars in this world are not poor in spirit. Even those who do not have money can still worship it as an idol in their heart. Mammon indeed usurps man's worship. We must discuss this matter in a thorough way. Mammon is an idol, and Christians must deal with mammon in a thorough way. This matter must be settled. (*The Collected Works of Watchman Nee*, vol. 59, pp. 71-72, 65-66)

Further Reading: The Collected Works of Watchman Nee, vol. 59, ch. 8

Enlightenment and inspiration: _____

_____

_____

_____

Morning Nourishment

Luke **How difficult it is for those who have riches to go**
18:24b **into the kingdom of God.**
  25 **For it is easier for a camel to enter through the eye
of a needle than for a rich man to enter into the
kingdom of God.**

Today's Reading

Second, being delivered from mammon is a part of our salvation. We have to show the brothers and sisters, according to the New Testament, first that mammon is an idol, and second that we have been delivered from mammon. Deliverance from mammon is part of our salvation. It is like deliverance from sin, the world, and the flesh. Many people know that in order to be saved, a man must be delivered from sin, from God's punishment, and from the world's bondage, but many people do not know that salvation includes deliverance from mammon. In Luke 18 and 19, three things—eternal life, the kingdom of the heavens, and salvation—are linked together. All three things relate to mammon. First, the young ruler wanted to inherit eternal life. The Lord told him to sell all that he had and to follow Him. Second, the Lord spoke on the difficulty of a rich man's entry into God's kingdom. It is easier for a camel to go through a needle's eye than for a rich man to enter God's kingdom! He went on to say that those who give up houses, wives, or children for the kingdom's sake would receive a hundredfold in this age and eternal life in the age to come. An entry into God's kingdom requires the forsaking of one's all. Peter was saved because he forsook his all. Those who are able to avoid the fate of a camel which has difficulty passing through a needle's eye are the ones who have forsaken their all to enter the kingdom of the heavens. Third, Zaccheus gave half of his possessions to the poor, and the Lord said that salvation had come to his house. Therefore, in order for a man to receive eternal life, the kingdom, and salvation, he has to be delivered from mammon and to dispose of everything.

Today we are not doing a fund-raising work. We are here to help others to receive eternal life, to enter the kingdom, and to be saved. If we ask many people if they want the kingdom, they will say yes. If we ask them if they want eternal life, they will also say yes. If we ask them if they want to be saved, they will say yes all the more. If, however, we ask if they want to be delivered from mammon, they will say no. A brother from a denomination came to our meetings, and said to my brother Hwai-zhu, "You are very good at fund-raising here at Hardoon Road." My brother asked why he was so interested in the saints' consecration. He answered, "I want to learn and observe a few more times. If your method works well, we will do the same in our denomination." This man only saw how money was offered. He did not see how we teach men to be delivered from mammon.

When Peter heard the Lord's word concerning a camel going through a needle's eye being easier than a rich man entering God's kingdom, he asked, "Then who can be saved?" He forgot that he himself was a camel, and that this camel, in fact, had passed through the needle's eye already. He forgot that there were eleven other camels who had done the same. While there is nothing harder than a rich man being saved, what is impossible with man is possible with God. The rich young ruler turned back. He was not a sinner or an evil man. He was charming and godly, yet he was not saved. (*The Collected Works of Watchman Nee*, vol. 59, pp. 67-68)

Further Reading: The Collected Works of Watchman Nee, vol. 59, ch. 8

Enlightenment and inspiration: _____

_____

_____

_____

_____

_____

_____

Morning Nourishment

Luke   And Zaccheus stood and said to the Lord, Behold,
19:8   the half of my possessions, Lord, I give to the poor,
       and if I have taken anything from anyone by false
       accusation, I restore four times as much.
Phil. And you yourselves also know, Philippians, that in
4:15,17 the beginning of the gospel, when I went out from
       Macedonia, no church had fellowship with me in
       the account of giving and receiving except you
       only....Not that I seek the gift, but I seek the fruit
       which increases to your account.

Today's Reading

Zaccheus was also a rich man. He was a slave of mammon, yet he was saved. He climbed up and down the tree. His going up and coming down undid him; it made him poor; nevertheless, he was saved. The young ruler is an example of what is "impossible with men," and Zaccheus is an example of what is "possible with God." A man experiences joy when his sins are forgiven. He experiences the same joy when he is delivered from mammon. When a man believes in the Lord, he finds peace in his heart. When mammon no longer occupies any place in him, he also finds peace in his heart. The receiving of eternal life is something that God accomplishes. Deliverance from mammon is also something that God accomplishes. Forgiveness of sins, the receiving of eternal life, and deliverance from mammon are all God's accomplishments. Peter asked, "Then who can be saved?" The Lord could have answered him, saying, "Zaccheus!" When God works in us, we will no longer remain a camel; we will be saved from mammon. Our salvation includes salvation from mammon. We should never leave out this item in our consideration of the sphere of our salvation.

Third, we have to learn to be rich before the Lord. He wants us to sell our all, but He does not want us to be in poverty. He wants us to learn to be rich in Him. As Christians, we are rich men, depending on the ground upon which we stand. In 1926 or 1927 I heard a pastor who said, "...While a believer should not be prosperous, he should at least be modestly well-off." Actually, according to the Bible God wants us all to be rich before Him and poor before the world. Only those who are poor on earth can be rich before God. When we are asked to sell our all, we are not being asked to spend all of our money, but to transfer it from our earthly bank to the heavenly bank. We are being asked to change our deposit from one place to another. Selling our all is making a transfer and depositing our money in heaven. Christians can be foolish indeed. When God asks, "Do you believe that it is safe to keep your mammon in the Bank of Shanghai?", we will answer, "Yes." When God asks, "Do you believe in the heavenly bank?", we will answer, "No." We do not deposit our money in the heavenly bank simply because the interest is higher there. God does not attract us with interest. Our Father, the rich One, is able to pay us one hundred dollars interest for every dollar we deposit. Our heavenly bank has an interest rate of ten thousand percent. There is a profit of ten thousand percent. Today it would be sensational if a bank offered three percent interest for any deposit. However, God is asking whether we have faith. He offers a profit of ten thousand percent. Our money has been in the earthly bank. We can invest in an earthly bank, but will we invest in God's eternal bank? Do we want to deposit our money in an eternal account? We are here to serve God! If we see this, we will give our all for this. In the past we gave our all to mammon; we served it. Now we have to put everything on God's side and serve Him. We have to be those who are rich in God. (*The Collected Works of Watchman Nee,* vol. 59, pp. 68-69)

Further Reading: The Collected Works of Watchman Nee, vol. 59, ch. 8

Enlightenment and inspiration: _____

_____

_____

_____

Morning Nourishment

Acts And they sold their properties and possessions
2:45 and divided them to all, as anyone had need.
2 Cor. As it is written, "He who *gathered* much had no
8:15 excess, and he who *gathered* little had no lack."

Today's Reading

Fourth, in the Gospels the Lord dealt with mammon by
ordering it to be given to the poor. During Pentecost the poor
referred to those who were in the church, the household of
the faith. When believers sell their all, they should lay the
proceeds at the feet of the elders and the apostles, rather than
give it immediately to the poor. On the one hand, we should
distribute our wealth to the poor outside the church, and
on the other hand, we should distribute it to those in the
church. There is much benefit in taking care of the unbeliev-
ing poor; this can expand our heart's capacity. Today we have
the church, and there are two distinct advantages to practicing giving in the church. First, the givers become men who
are delivered from mammon. Second, the receivers are believ-
ing brothers and sisters. The Lord told men to sell their all
because He did not want men to fall into the bondage of mammon. He wanted men to serve Him....A Christian should
never accumulate mammon. We have to consider mammon as
a venomous snake; it is not simply a bug or an ant. We have to
shake off mammon like Paul shook off the viper. It is for our
own good that we sell our all.

The twelve apostles sold their all and gave up everything.
At Pentecost, Peter did not give a message on giving one's all,
but when the three thousand saw the twelve who had sold
their all, they did the same thing. In Acts 4, another five thousand came in. They saw the three thousand who had sold
their all, and they did the same thing. Those in the succeeding
generation take their example from the previous generation.
The five thousand followed the example of the three thousand, the three thousand followed the example of the twelve,

and the twelve followed the example of Christ. What we hear can never match what we see. When men come to the church, we want them to see love and oneness, but they should also see that we have sold our all. If we do not set the standard right, the next generation will have no way to go on. Whatever we want our next generation to be, we have to be this in our generation. Today we are in the recovery; we are here to bear the responsibility of the recovery. May we be those who take the way of voluntary poverty.

Fifth, we must uphold and maintain the practice of "He who gathered much had no excess" (2 Cor. 8:15). After we have handed over our all, we will gain new possessions gradually. We do not expect to gather much when we sow; we simply let go when we sow. Nevertheless, it is a fact that we will gather much. What then should we do? Second Corinthians 8 and 9 come after Acts 2 and 4, not before. In 2 Corinthians, we find the words *He who gathered much had no excess.* This is not a question of whether a man has sold his all, but a question of what a man does after he has sold his all. We have to empty ourselves of everything at least once, but as new income is received, we have to empty again. As God blesses us and increases our income, we surely have to pour out more. Those who sow abundantly should not be in excess. The more absolutely a person deals with the matter of mammon, the faster his money will come back to him. A brother once remarked, "We can never beat God in His work."...No matter how much income we receive, God wants us to maintain the practice of not having excess. We must deal with money in an absolute way. Before the Lord, we must continually give away our money. (*The Collected Works of Watchman Nee*, vol. 59, pp. 69-71)

Further Reading: The Collected Works of Watchman Nee, vol. 59, ch. 8

Enlightenment and inspiration: _____

_____

_____

_____

Morning Nourishment

Exo. And the LORD gave the people favor in the sight of
12:36 the Egyptians, so that they lent unto them *such
things as they required:* and they spoiled the Egyptians.
Col. 3:5 Put to death therefore your members which are on
the earth:...greediness, which is idolatry.

Today's Reading

When the Israelites left Egypt, they took all the money
with them (Exo. 12:36). When they crossed the Red Sea, the
money crossed over with them. Any money that was left in
Egypt, regardless of how much it was, was useless. Only those
who have passed the Red Sea can employ their money to the
proper use for the building up of the tabernacle. What is
needed first is for the person himself to be delivered. Second,
the money has to follow. Then third, there is the building up
of the tabernacle....The sin of the golden calf must first be
exposed, and a person must first be delivered from such sin,
before the question of the gold can be settled....The gold
should have been given to the tabernacle. But because of idolatry, the gold went to the calf. Hence, the worship of the golden
calf was not only a matter of sin, but a loss for the tabernacle.
It was the same gold. But when it was placed on the golden
calf, it was wrong, and it had to be ground into powder. On the
contrary, when it was placed in the tabernacle, it was right.
The same material could be directed toward different objects.
One object was the idol. The other object was the tabernacle.
In the New Testament...idolatry is linked to covetousness
(Col. 3:5). Where there is deliverance from idolatry, there is
deliverance from money. (*The Resumption of Watchman Nee's
Ministry,* vol. 1, pp. 291-292)

All things are created by God. God is the unique source of
all things; He is above all things. When men see all things,
they should be moved to worship God...."All things" are
diverse and complicated. Satan wants to unify all things.

There is no way to add up all things. For example, a chair and a table cannot be added together to make one unit. What is an adult plus a child plus a piece of luggage plus a bar of gold plus a piece of land? They do not add up to one unit. However, if you convert all these things into money, you can add them up. If all things cannot be unified, how can the businessmen do their accounting? With so many different units, how can one reckon their values? Money is the only means by which we can reckon all things. With money, a piece of land becomes no more a piece of land; it becomes money. Rice becomes no more rice; it becomes money. When we add together all things, we end up with a certain amount of money. In the end, Revelation 18 tells us that even the human soul can be reckoned with money. When a man sells his time to work for others, he is selling his soul. For example, when I hire a laborer, I agree with him ahead of time how much I will pay him for working eight hours. This is to buy the human soul with money. Money can buy us the human soul, and money can buy us all things. God created the earth, yet man divided it up into pieces and reckoned the value of every piece with money....In six days, God created all things. Can you find out how much money "all things" are worth? Here are all sorts of things, in all fashions and colors. Yet Satan has simplified these things and unified them under money. This is why money is called in Chinese "the common goods."

If a person truly wants to serve the Lord, he must be delivered from money. Once a person's thoughts are turned to money, he cannot serve God. It is wrong for a man to view all things from the side of money; he should view all things from the side of God. (*The Resumption of Watchman Nee's Ministry*, vol. 2, pp. 500-501)

Further Reading: The Resumption of Watchman Nee's Ministry,
    vol. 2, ch. 65, pp. 499-501

Enlightenment and inspiration: _____

_____

_____

_____

_____

Morning Nourishment

Matt. Then He said to them, Render then the things that
22:21b are Caesar's to Caesar and the things that are God's
to God.

1 Tim. For the love of money is a root of all evils, *because*
6:10 *of* which some, aspiring after *money*, have been led
away from the faith and pierced themselves through
with many pains.

Today's Reading

Satan reduces all things into one kind of thing. This one
thing is money. There is nothing in this world that cannot
be bought with money. If a person has money, he has all
things....All things are created by God. Only money is not created by God; it comes from Caesar. When men asked Christ if
there was a need to pay tribute money, He asked them to show
Him a denarius, and He answered, "Render then the things
that are Caesar's to Caesar" (Matt. 22:21). He did not take any
money out from His own pocket. Had He done this, others
would have said that He too had Caesar in His pocket.

When we gain God, we have all things. In the same way,
when Satan takes hold of money, he has everything. Money
is omnipotent; everything can be bought with money. To buy
wood, stones, or any other things that we like, we need mammon. In this way, mammon becomes the power, the center of
man's worship. Is man going to worship God or mammon? This
becomes the controversy of the universe. The worship of God
lies on one side of all things, and the worship of mammon lies
on the other side of all things. Mammon is diametrically
opposed to God. Why can mammon withstand God? It is
because it is the only thing that can unify all things. Covetousness is not only a root of all evils (1 Tim. 6:10); it is even the
same as idolatry. Riches are an idol. The Bible says that covetousness and idolatry are the same kind of sins (Eph. 5:5). After
a man is saved, if he has not dealt with his money in a clear way,
he is not yet fully saved. If a person still keeps wooden or stone

idols in his house, will we accept such a one for baptism? Yet, many people have never dealt with the matter of money after they are saved. Today, we say that India is a nation of idols and that there are more idols than people in that land. Yet, there are countless more people today who worship mammon than people who worship idols. From the people in Asia to those in Africa, from the scientists to the most superstitious people, everyone worships mammon. Mammon is the most common object of worship.

God wants to gain us, and mammon also wants to gain us. Unless God's people are delivered from the power of mammon, they will not have a proper testimony and cannot be proper Christians. If a man tries to hold on to both sides, he will not be able to serve the Lord well. Why did the Lord put such a harsh requirement upon the young ruler and ask him to sell all he had? That young man was quite good and had kept all the laws. But the Lord said that he lacked one thing, the most important thing, which had to do with mammon (Luke 18:18-23).

In church history, the Moravian church was the group that had the strongest mission. Its founder, Count Zinzendorf, gave up all his possessions for the Lord....A few decades ago, seven Englishmen came to China to preach the gospel. They were known as the Cambridge Seven. Among them was C. T. Studd, who was a cricket champion. He had received an inheritance of two hundred fifty thousand pounds, which equals 1.2 million U.S. dollars, and he gave it all away. When he told the British Consulate that he was going to China, the Consulate General was shocked by his consecration and dared not accept his application. After a week, Mr. Studd was still firm concerning his decision. God could use Mr. Studd in a great way because he had overcome mammon. (*The Resumption of Watchman Nee's Ministry,* vol. 2, pp. 396-399)

Further Reading: The Resumption of Watchman Nee's Ministry, vol. 2, ch. 54, pp. 395-399

Enlightenment and inspiration: _____

_____

_____

_____

Hymns, #437

1 Hast thou heard Him, seen Him, known Him?
   Is not thine a captured heart?
   Chief among ten thousand own Him;
   Joyful choose the better part.

   Captivated by His beauty,
   Worthy tribute haste to bring;
   Let His peerless worth constrain thee,
   Crown Him now unrivaled King.

2 Idols once they won thee, charmed thee,
      Lovely things of time and sense;
   Gilded thus does sin disarm thee,
      Honeyed lest thou turn thee thence.

3 What has stripped the seeming beauty
      From the idols of the earth?
   Not a sense of right or duty,
      But the sight of peerless worth.

4 Not the crushing of those idols,
      With its bitter void and smart;
   But the beaming of His beauty,
      The unveiling of His heart.

5 Who extinguishes their taper
      Till they hail the rising sun?
   Who discards the garb of winter
      Till the summer has begun?

6 'Tis that look that melted Peter,
      'Tis that face that Stephen saw,
   'Tis that heart that wept with Mary,
      Can alone from idols draw:

7 Draw and win and fill completely,
      Till the cup o'erflow the brim;
   What have we to do with idols
      Who have companied with Him?

Composition for prophecy with main point and sub-points: _____

_____

_____

_____

_____

_____

_____

_____

_____

_____

_____

_____

_____

_____

_____

_____

_____

_____

_____

_____

_____

_____

_____

_____

_____

_____

_____

_____

_____

_____

_____

_____

_____

_____

_____

_____

_____

_____

Morning Nourishment

Matt.   No one can serve two masters, for either he will
6:24   hate the one and love the other, or he will hold to
        one and despise the other. You cannot serve God
        and mammon.

Today's Reading

Mammon stands in opposition to God. For this reason,
every child of God has to overcome the power of mammon.
If anyone does not overcome its power, he will have no spiritual power. The power of mammon does not lie in how much
mammon a person possesses. Its power on the poor may be
stronger than its power on the rich.

When we offer up all our money and then receive it back
again from the Lord, the money will be very different. Formerly, we were the masters. Now we become the stewards.
If we are a steward, yet waste our master's money, the Lord's
illustration says aptly that some will accuse us (Luke 16:1).
They will say that we are wasting our master's money. Today,
we may hold different standards of living. But the principle
remains the same: We have to do our best to be frugal.

Once the problem of money is settled, we will become a
broad person. Today everyone's mind is different....When we
speak of the need of the church, different people have different thoughts and reactions. When some hear about the need
of the church, they will say that it is all right to buy less land
and build smaller buildings; they think that there is no need
to be very serious about the matter. A person who is not serious will not do things in a serious way. However, we cannot
consider matters from our point of view. We have to consider
matters from God's point of view. Once the problem of mammon is settled, we will be enlarged. A man cannot serve two
masters. Either he serves the Lord, or he serves mammon.
The reason we are in darkness and are not in the light is that
there is the entanglement of money. If we can solve this problem, many other problems will be solved.

The gospel has been "bottled up" like water kept in a bottle, and money is like the cork of the bottle. If money does not go away, water will not come. If you do not give away your money, you will not even be able to live a proper human life. A person has to open his eyelids before he can see. In the same way, if money does not go away, a person cannot see the Lord.

I know that many brothers here are more well off than brothers in other localities. In other localities, some people cannot even send their children to school. We can be in scarcity, but we cannot become small. We cannot become small just through our scarcity. We have to show other brothers that not one thing is our own.

What we want is first you, and then yours. I am a priest, and I live for God. We care only for the fact of handing ourselves over and not for argument. We are not here for money; we are here to help others to hand themselves over. If a man does not hand himself over, it is meaningless to receive a few dollars from him; it is better to return such money back to him. God would not be pleased with such money. In God's eyes, money is not the main problem. A man hands over his money because he has first handed over himself. You as a person are more important than your money. When a person comes, what he has will come along with him.

We have to look to the Lord to bring all the saints...into this practice. Otherwise, our words here for the last few days will result only in a few more consecrations. In another five days, things will cool down again. This is indeed a serious matter. If we can bring the brothers and sisters into this practice, many tremendous things will follow. (*The Resumption of Watchman Nee's Ministry,* vol. 2, pp. 399, 407-409)

Further Reading: The Resumption of Watchman Nee's Ministry,
    vol. 2, ch. 54, pp. 404-409

Enlightenment and inspiration: _____

_____

_____

Morning Nourishment

Matt. For where your treasure is, there will your heart be
6:21 also.
31-33 Therefore do not be anxious, saying, What shall we
eat? or, What shall we drink? or, With what shall
we be clothed? For all these things the Gentiles are
anxiously seeking. For your heavenly Father knows
that you need all these things. But seek first His
kingdom and His righteousness, and all these things
will be added to you.

Today's Reading

After a person has sold everything, he will still receive
income; money will still find its way back to his hand. How
should he manage his money? Even after a person has offered
up all of his money, we should not think that money will no
longer have an influence on him. Some people can give away
their money all at once, but money can gradually regain its
power over them. Eventually, they will consider their money
to be their own once again. Therefore, a believer must learn to
continually let go of his money.

The Christian way of managing wealth is completely different from that of an unbeliever. The Christian way of financial management is the way of giving. The unbeliever's way
is the way of accumulating. Today we are concerned with how
a Christian should live in order to be free from want. God has
promised us that we will have no lack on earth. The birds
of the air have no lack of food, and the flowers of the field
have no lack of clothing. Even so God's children should have
no lack of clothing and food. If they have any lack, there must
be a reason or cause for it. If a brother is financially hard-
pressed, he is not managing his wealth according to God's
principle.

After you have forsaken all of your possessions to follow
the Lord, you should walk according to God's principle. If
you do not follow God's principle, you will eventually end up in

poverty. There is a great need for many of God's children to learn to manage their wealth. If they do not learn to manage their wealth, they should expect nothing except hardship in the way ahead of them. (*The Collected Works of Watchman Nee,* vol. 49, pp. 419-420)

Our God is a rich God. He does not need our money. The cattle of a thousand hills and the goats of ten thousand mountains are His. All the gold and silver are His. Then why does He need our money? It is because where our treasure is, there will our heart be also (Matt. 6:21). Money is a material thing that belongs to the earth. Yet the Bible puts God and mammon together. This proves that man's heart is either touched by God or by money. God's test of a man's heart toward Him is in the way of man's giving. Hmm

I started working for the Lord sixteen years ago in 1922. Although I cannot say that my work has been perfect, I can say that all the shortages have been covered under the blood. Sometimes I gave one-tenth, sometimes two-tenths, and sometimes five-tenths of what I received. Because there was never a steady flow of income, it was difficult to determine ahead of time how much I should give. But I can say that the times when I felt the pain of giving the most were the times that my thanksgivings and praises were the loudest....I despise anyone who says that he is living by faith, but who knows only how to receive but not to give. Sometimes the best test of where a person stands is to consider his giving. A worker of the Lord must give at least one-tenth, because the Bible shows us that the Levites had to tithe the same way as the rest of the Israelites (Num. 18:25-29). (*The Collected Works of Watchman Nee,* vol. 43, pp. 726-727)

Further Reading: The Collected Works of Watchman Nee, vol. 43, ch. 85

Enlightenment and inspiration: _____

_____

_____

_____

_____

_____

Morning Nourishment

1 Cor.   Now concerning the collection for the saints, just
16:1-2   as I directed the churches of Galatia, so you also do.
         On the first day of the week each one of you should
         lay aside in store to himself whatever he may have
         been prospered, that no collections be made when
         I come.

Luke   Give, and it will be given to you; a good measure,
6:38   pressed down, shaken together, *and* running over,
       they will give into your bosom. For with what mea-
       sure you measure, it shall be measured to you in
       return.

Today's Reading

If we do not give, we are being unrighteous. The rent and
utilities of the meeting hall all cost money. If we do not give,
we are not doing our part, and others are paying for us to sit
here. This is unrighteousness, and unrighteousness is sin.
Do not think that others do not know and that we can cheat.
God knows.

Many people are familiar with the meeting in Acts 20:7,
but they have forgotten the giving in 1 Corinthians 16. At
that time Paul asked the Corinthian believers to give because
the Jerusalem believers were lacking. Today we do not send
money to Jerusalem, but there are many local saints who are
in need. First Corinthians 16:2 says, "You should." This means
that whatever is spoken of is an injunction and a command.
Paul said, "On the first day of the week each one of you should
lay aside in store to himself whatever he may have been prospered." This means that we should set aside portions of our
income ahead of time. Of all the money that we receive,
we should designate a portion which cannot be touched.
Every time we receive anything, we should set aside a portion
for giving. (*The Collected Works of Watchman Nee,* vol. 43,
pp. 727-728)

As believers we have to look to the Lord for our food, clothing, and other needs while we live on earth today. Without God's mercy, we cannot pass through our days on earth. This is true even for the rich ones; they have to look to the Lord also....Those who trust in the Lord may not have much in the way of savings, but the Lord will not leave them in difficulties. He can supply all their needs. However, we must also realize that God's supply is with conditions.

If God can feed the birds in the air, He can keep us alive. In reality, no one can feed all the birds or supply enough fertilizer to grow all the lilies of the field. But God has enough riches to keep the birds of the air and the lilies of the field alive. He also has enough riches to keep His children alive. God does not want to see us come short in anything. He does not want our living to be deprived in any way. Everyone who falls into deprivation falls because he has a problem in himself; he has not managed his wealth according to God's way. If we manage our money according to God's law, we will not be in poverty.

Luke 6:38...describes the type of person God will supply.... If everything belongs to Him, why are God's children poor? Why do His children experience lack? It is not because God cannot supply. Rather, we need to meet His requirements before we can receive His supply. We need to meet certain conditions before our prayers can be answered. Even our salvation had certain requirements to it—we had to believe. Every promise has conditions, and we must fulfill these conditions before we can receive the promise. Likewise, we need to fulfill God's requirements before we can receive His supply. His requirement is to give. The Lord says, "Give, and it will be given to you." (*The Collected Works of Watchman Nee*, vol. 49, pp. 420-421)

Further Reading: The Collected Works of Watchman Nee, vol. 49, ch. 28

Enlightenment and inspiration: _____

_____

_____

_____

_____

Morning Nourishment

Acts In all things I have shown you by example that toil-
20:35 ing in this way we ought to support the weak and
to remember the words of the Lord Jesus, that He
Himself said, It is more blessed to give than to
receive.

Today's Reading

I have seen a few brothers and sisters who fell into dire need
because they were unfaithful in the matter of giving. They
were not actually lacking in income. The Bible shows us a fun-
damental principle—one must give to become rich and one
becomes poor by accumulating riches. Whoever cares only for
himself is destined to be in poverty. Whoever learns to give is
destined to have riches. God's Word says it, and it is true. If we
want to escape poverty, we have to give again and again. The
more we give, the more God will give to us. Since we are willing
to share our surplus with others, others will also be happy to
share their surplus with us in the future. If we give one-twentieth to others, others will also give one-twentieth to us. If we give
one-thousandth to others, others will also give one-thousandth
to us.

With what measure we measure to others, with the same
measure others will measure to us. In what capacity we treat
our brothers and sisters, with the same capacity God will treat
us. If we are willing to sacrifice our livelihood, others will also
sacrifice their livelihood for us. If we only give others that
which is totally useless, things which we never use, others will
certainly give us totally useless and unusable things. Many
people have problems with their income because they have
problems with their giving. If a person has no problem with his
giving, it is hard to imagine that he will have problems with his
income. God's Word is quite clear. If we give to others, the Lord
will give to us. If we do not give to others, the Lord will not give
to us. Most people only exercise faith when they ask God for
money; they do not exercise faith in giving money. It is no

wonder that they have no faith to receive anything from God.

Brothers, as soon as we become Christians, we have to learn the basic lesson of financial stewardship. Christians have a unique way of managing their wealth: What we receive depends on what we give. In other words, the Christian way of financial stewardship is to receive according to what we give. Worldly people give according to what they have received, but we receive according to what we give. Our inflow depends on our outflow. Those who crave money and cling to it can never receive God's money; they will never receive any supply from God.

We should all look to the Lord for our needs, but God will supply the needs of only one type of people—those who give. The words *good measure,* which the Lord uses in Luke 6:38, are wonderful words. When God gives to man, He is never stingy. He is ever generous and overflowing. Our God is always generous. Our God's cup is always running over. God is never petty....Our God is such a generous God. He gives by pressing down, shaking together, heaping up, and running over. However, He also says that with what measure we measure to others, it will be measured to us in return. If we are shrewd and exact in giving to others, God will only touch others to give to us in a shrewd and exact way.

We must give first to others, before others will give to us. Most people never learn to give. They always want God to answer their prayers. We have to give first before we can receive. If we have not received anything recently, it means that we have a problem in giving. I have been a Christian for more than twenty years, and I can surely bear witness to this principle. Whenever a person has a problem with his giving, he will experience a lack. (*The Collected Works of Watchman Nee,* vol. 49, pp. 421-422)

Further Reading: The Collected Works of Watchman Nee, vol. 49, ch. 28

Enlightenment and inspiration: _____

_____

_____

_____

Morning Nourishment

Phil. Not that I seek the gift, but I seek the fruit which
4:17-19 increases to your account. But I have received in
full all things and abound; I have been filled, receiving from Epaphroditus the things from you, a
sweet-smelling savor, an acceptable sacrifice, well-
pleasing to God. And my God will fill your every
need according to His riches, in glory, in Christ
Jesus.

Today's Reading

The Corinthians were parsimonious in giving, while the
Philippians were very generous. Paul received from the Philippians time and again. He told the Philippians, "My God will
fill your every need according to His riches, in glory, in Christ
Jesus."...Paul emphasized, "*My God* will fill your every need."
The God who receives the money and the gifts will supply the
needs of the givers.

God will never supply those who do not give. Today many
people hold on to Philippians 4:19, but they do not really
understand it, because God does not supply those who ask,
but those who give. Only those who give can claim Philippians
4:19. Those who do not give cannot claim this promise. You
must give before you can say, "O God, today supply all my
needs according to Your riches in Christ Jesus." God supplied
all the needs for only the Philippians. God will only supply the
needs of those who are practicing the principle of giving.

When your vessel is empty of flour and when your bottle is
empty of oil, please remember that you must first make bread
for Elijah with what little you have left....Take the little oil
and flour and make bread for the prophet first....Who has
ever heard of a bottle of oil feeding a person for three and a
half years? But let me tell you, if you take your little flour and
oil and make bread for the prophet, you will find the bottle of
oil feeding you for three and a half years (cf. Luke 4:25-26;
1 Kings 17:8-16). What one has may not be enough to feed him

even once. But when it is given away, it becomes the means of one's livelihood. This is the Christian way of financial management.

Both the New Testament and the Old Testament teach us the same thing. The Christian way should not be the way of poverty. God does not want us to be poor. If there is poverty or want among us, it is because some people are holding back their money. The more you love yourself, the more you will go hungry. The more importance you attach to money, the poorer you will become....The more one holds back his money, the more miserable and depleted he becomes. This is a sure principle. During the past twenty years, I have seen many such cases. I only wish that we could release our money and allow it to circulate around the earth, to work, and to become part of God's miracles and answers to prayers. Then when we have needs, God will supply us.

Not only are we in God's hands, but Satan is also in His hands. The cattle on a thousand hills and the sheep on ten thousand hills are His. Only foolish ones think that they have earned their own money. A new believer must see that tithing is our duty. We should give what we earn to take care of the poor saints. Do not be so foolish as to always receive. Do not try to save up your money or hide it away. The Christian way is the way of giving. Always give what you have, and you will find money becoming something living in the church. When you have any need, the birds in the air will work for you, and God will perform miracles for you.

Cast yourself upon the Word of God. Otherwise, God cannot carry out His word in you. First give yourself to God, and then give your money again and again. If you do this, God will have the opportunity to give to you. (*The Collected Works of Watchman Nee,* vol. 49, pp. 432-434)

Further Reading: The Collected Works of Watchman Nee, vol. 49, ch. 28

Enlightenment and inspiration: _____

_____

_____

_____

Morning Nourishment

Matt. But take care not to do your righteousness before
6:1-4 men in order to be gazed at by them; otherwise,
you have no reward with your Father who is in the
heavens. Therefore when you give alms, do not
sound a trumpet before you as the hypocrites do
in the synagogues and in the streets, so that they
may be glorified by men. Truly I say to you, They
have their reward in full. But you, when you give
alms, do not let your left hand know what your
right hand is doing, so that your alms may be in
secret; and your Father who sees in secret will
repay you.

Today's Reading

Man's flesh, seeking to glorify itself, always wants to do
good deeds before men to be praised by them. But the kingdom people, who live in an emptied and humbled spirit and
walk in a pure and single heart under the heavenly ruling of
the kingdom, are not allowed to do anything in the flesh for
the praise of men, but must do all things in the spirit for the
pleasing of their heavenly Father.

We must do our righteous deeds in secret, for our Father is
in secret. In verse 4 the Lord says that our Father sees in
secret. The kingdom people as children of the heavenly Father
must live in the presence of the Father and care for the
Father's presence. Whatever they do in secret for the Father's
kingdom, the Father sees in secret. The heavenly Father's
seeing in secret must be an incentive to doing their righteous
deeds in secret. In this verse the Lord also said that the
Father will repay us. This may transpire in this age (2 Cor.
9:10-11) or in the coming age as a reward (Luke 14:14).

The effect of doing our righteous deeds in secret is that
the self and the flesh are killed. If people in society today are
not allowed to make a show of their good deeds, they will not
do them. As long as people have an opportunity to make a

public display of their righteous deeds, they are glad to perform them. This is the deplorable practice of today's degraded Christianity, especially in the matter of fund raising, which provides an excellent opportunity for the donors to make a display. The greater the public show, the more money people are willing to give. Certainly such making of a show is of the flesh. Giving alms to the poor in order to show how generous you are is not a matter of anger, lust, or the natural being; it is a matter of the self, the flesh. Making a show in such a way is simply boasting for yourself. Thus, for us kingdom people, a basic principle concerning righteous deeds is never to make a show of ourselves. As much as possible, hide yourself, keep yourself covered, and do things in secret. We should be so hidden that, as the Lord Jesus says, our left hand does not know what our right hand is doing (Matt. 6:3). This means that we should not let others know what we are doing.

No matter what kind of righteous deeds we do—giving material things to the saints, praying, fasting, doing something to please God—we must try our best to do them in secret. If your righteous deeds are in secret, you may be assured that you are growing in life and are healthy. But at any time you exhibit yourself in your righteous deeds, you are not healthy. Such an exhibition greatly frustrates your growth in life.

The universe indicates that God is hidden, that God is secret. Although He has done a great many things, people are not aware that He has done them. We may have seen the things done by God, but none of us has ever seen Him, for He is always hidden, always secret. God's life is of such a secret and hidden nature....This is the nature of the kingdom people in the doing of their righteous deeds. (*Life-study of Matthew*, pp. 258-259, 261-262)

Further Reading: Life-study of Matthew, msg. 21, pp. 257-264

Enlightenment and inspiration: _____

_____

_____

_____

_____

Hymns, #452

1 Tell me not of earthly pleasures,
   Tempt me not with sordid gain;
Mock me not with earth's illusions,
   Vex me not with honors vain.
I am weaned from sinful idols;
   I am henceforth not my own;
I have given my heart to Jesus,
   I belong to Him alone.

   I am not my own,
   I am not my own.
   I belong to Jesus,
   And I am not my own.

2 Oh, the blessed rest it brings us
   To belong to Christ alone;
We can draw on all His fulness
   When we've nothing of our own.
Blessed Jesus, take me, own me,
   Make me, keep me wholly Thine.
Deign to find in me Thy portion,
   While I joy to call Thee mine.

3 Weary soul, give up the struggle,
   Cease at length thyself to own;
Give yourself away to Jesus,
   And belong to Him alone.
Once He gave His all to win thee,
   Now He asks as much of thee;
All He has He fully gives thee;
   Let thy love His portion be.

*Composition for prophecy with main point and
sub-points:* _____

_____

_____

_____

_____

_____

_____

_____

_____

_____

_____

_____

_____

_____

_____

_____

_____

_____

_____

_____

_____

_____

_____

_____

_____

_____

_____

_____

_____

_____

_____

_____

_____

Morning Nourishment

Phil. But I have received in full all things and abound;
4:18 I have been filled, receiving from Epaphroditus
the things from you, a sweet-smelling savor, an
acceptable sacrifice, well-pleasing to God.

Today's Reading

Sometimes God will ask a person to sell all he has. Sometimes He will only ask a person to give what he has in excess. Whatever it may be, the heart has to be released. In Acts, the apostle rebuked Ananias for keeping back what he had in excess (Acts 5:3-4)....If there is any excess, it should be given away.

Sister Eva said that every time she went to bed, she would always consider how she could save something more from her spending in order that others may receive more. We need to take care of our livelihood, and we need to take care of our family. But that is not this issue today. As long as we would set aside a portion from our income and would lower our standard of living a little, we will be able to give away all our excess.

Today, when we speak of handing ourselves over, we are not talking about what we have to do to take care of our money. Rather, we are saying that a person has to offer himself up for the Lord and for the gospel. Brothers and sisters who are engaged in an occupation, the Lord needs your ministry in your job! These few years we are short of new co-workers. Formerly, at its peak we had about four hundred co-workers. Today we only have about two hundred, with two hundred short. In order to fill up the gap of these two hundred workers, there must be a group of people who would go to make money. Formerly, I dared not say such a word. But today I dare to say such a word. Some should go to make money and offer their money to the Lord's service. They should consecrate themselves to make money for the Lord's service. Perhaps such a one can make a million dollars. He will only take what he needs to sustain his livelihood. The rest he will give to the church. If you are only a spectator here, nothing will happen to you. But if you want to give yourselves for the co-workers' need, it demands your life.

First He wants us; then He wants what is ours. We ourselves have to come to Him first before we can bring what we have to Him. If we do not come, God will not accept what we have. All the brothers and sisters have to see that everything is for the Lord and that everything has to center around the Lord. We must have the same center. Although some function in their money-making ministry while others function in their ministry of the word, the center for both must be the same. (*The Resumption of Watchman Nee's Ministry*, vol. 1, pp. 310-311)

The fragrant odor [in Philippians 4:18] refers to the sweet savor of the burnt offering (Gen. 8:20-21; Lev. 1:9). The offering we give to God's servants is not only a sacrifice to God, but also a fragrant odor of a burnt offering that is well-pleasing to Him. This reveals that the sacrifice here is like a burnt offering that is satisfying and well-pleasing to God.

By being offered to God for God's use by us who are of God, what was considered by God as "mammon of unrighteousness" (Luke 16:9), that is, as deceitful riches (Matt. 13:22) and uncertain riches (1 Tim. 6:17) which will fail (Luke 16:9), can actually become our "fellowship" with the saints, our "righteousness" toward men before God, an acceptable "sacrifice" to God, and a well-pleasing "sweet-smelling savor" to Him. Riches that deceive men, corrupt men, and destroy men can actually become such transcendent blessings that we have before God! This all depends on our offering of material riches. (*Life Lessons*, p. 187)

Further Reading: The Resumption of Watchman Nee's Ministry,
    vol. 1, pp. 309-312; *Life Lessons*, lsn. 24

Enlightenment and inspiration: _____

_____

_____

_____

_____

Morning Nourishment

2 Cor. For whether we were beside ourselves, *it was*
5:13 to God; or whether we are sober-minded, *it is* for
you.

Today's Reading

The Bible also tells us about many people who were beside
themselves in offering up their possessions and houses. Acts 4
mentions the disciples selling their all and laying the money
they received at the apostles' feet (vv. 34-35). Many people
agree that we should be zealous, but they say that we should be
careful, balanced, and not go to extremes. Yet throughout the
past two thousand years, all those who have truly consecrated
themselves to the Lord were men who risked everything to
offer up themselves. The more a person loves the Lord, the
more he consecrates. One brother asked me, "How can you love
the Lord so much, and why can't I love Him as much?" I said, "If
you give your money to the Lord, you will love Him. The Lord
said that where your treasure is, there is your heart also." If
you want your heart to follow the Lord, your money must first
go to the Lord. When your money goes into the offering box, and
you say, "Amen," your heart will go with it as well.

In Shanghai two sisters who were nurses each earned less
than a hundred dollars a month. They saved their wages in the
bank. After they heard the Lord's word, they were moved in
their heart, and one after the other offered up all their savings.

Today many people are planning too much for themselves.
They are not willing to offer up their all. They make reserva-
tions for themselves. The result is that the gospel has lost its
impact. During every great revival in history, we find men
who were beside themselves in loving the Lord, who risked all
to offer up themselves. I am not exhorting you to give everything to the Lord, but you must be a person who is fully consecrated to the Lord.

One elderly sister once came to Mr. George Müller and said,
"My seventieth birthday is approaching. By that time I will

have saved enough money to buy a coat. This has been my wish
for many years. I have been saving since I was forty-two years
old, and I have been looking forward to the day when I would
have such a coat. I have waited twenty-eight years. Today I can
finally buy it. However, the Lord is touching me to offer up
these fifteen pounds." When Mr. Müller heard this, he felt that
this would cost the elderly sister too much, and he wondered
whether she would later regret it. He dared not accept that
money. Yet the sister was quite resolute and determined to
offer it up. Later, Mr. Müller testified that he had thought that
it was difficult for poor people to love the Lord. But the Lord
had died for all, and when one was touched by the Lord, even a
savings of twenty-eight years meant nothing to her anymore.

Today we want all the young people to offer their time to the
Lord. At the same time, we want them to offer themselves fully
to the Lord. Some may have to give themselves to make money
for the Lord. Such ones have to do their best to earn and
offer....Some may have to offer themselves to serve the Lord
full-time. We need both kinds of people. Does not the gospel
need to be preached in many places? Is not the church taking
the right path? If there were no need to preach the gospel, and
if the church were on the wrong path, we could keep our money
and save it for our own use. But if the gospel needs to be
preached, and if the church is on the right path, we have to be
beside ourselves for the Lord. We have to recalibrate the focus of
our living. Formerly, we earned money for ourselves. Today
everything has to be for the Lord....We have to rise up and be
beside ourselves. We have to be beside ourselves in the preaching of the gospel and in offering up our all. (*The Collected Works
of Watchman Nee,* vol. 41, pp. 198-200)

Further Reading: The Collected Works of Watchman Nee, vol. 41,
    ch. 26

Enlightenment and inspiration: _____

_____

_____

_____

_____

Morning Nourishment

Mal.   Bring the whole tithe to the storehouse that there
3:10   may be food in My house; and prove Me, if you will,
       by this, says Jehovah of hosts, whether I will open
       to you the windows of heaven and pour out bless-
       ing for you until there is no room for it.

Heb.   Through Him then let us offer up a sacrifice of
13:15 praise continually to God, that is, the fruit of lips
       confessing His name.

16   But do not forget doing good and sharing *with
       others*, for with such sacrifices God is well pleased.

Today's Reading

In the Old Testament...the Israelites were in great poverty and difficulty. How could they carry out the words of
Malachi 3:10? The Israelites might have asked, "If we cannot
get by with ten loads of rice, how can we get by with nine?
If ten bags of flour are insufficient, how can nine bags be sufficient?" These are words out of a carnal and foolish mouth. God
reproached the people and told them that what is impossible
with man is possible with God.

Ten loads are the reason for poverty, while nine loads are
the cause for abundance. Man thinks that the more he has in
his hand, the better off he will be. However, keeping things
in one's hand is the very cause for poverty, while offering
things to God is the very cause for blessing. If I have an additional load in my hands, it will become my curse. But if it is put
in God's storehouse, it becomes my blessing....When you hold
something back, you end up in poverty. (*The Collected Works
of Watchman Nee,* vol. 49, p. 431)

The "tithe" [in Malachi 3:10] is the legal amount of offering
which God required from the harvest of the Israelites....This
word superabundantly displays the infinitely rich promise of
God. Although it was spoken to the Israelites in the Old Testament, in principle it applies also to the New Testament believers. If we will fully offer to God what belongs to Him that the

church may be richly supplied, God will open the windows of heaven for us and pour out a blessing to us, which there will not be enough room to contain. (*Life Lessons*, p. 183)

Two sacrifices are spoken of [in Hebrews 13:15-16]. The first is the sacrifice of praise, and the second is that of doing good and sharing with others. A sacrifice is something that is a loss to oneself and a gain to God. A sacrifice of praise is a praise that is rendered to God at one's own loss. A sacrifice of sharing or giving is giving something to God at one's own expense.

We do not have adequate praise in the bread-breaking meeting because we fall short in sharing and giving. We must give to the extent that we "feel" our giving. In other words, we have to give to the extent that we can sense the loss. Only this kind of offering can be considered a sacrifice. When we do this, we will spontaneously offer up the sacrifice of praise. If we give in a casual way, our praise will not be high. If we do not have the sacrifice of giving, we will not have the sacrifice of praise....In addition to the sacrifice of praise, there is still something that follows. The phrase "do not forget" refers to the fact that it is most easy for men to forget....We should not forget doing good and sharing with others.

Praise and giving are like two legs. If one is shorter than the other, we cannot expect a person to walk properly. Praise and giving are also like two wings. If one is missing, a bird cannot fly. It may still have one wing, but the wing is useless. A bird with only one wing cannot fly. When we come to the meeting, we sometimes find superficial ones uttering a few words of praise, but their praise is never high. (*The Collected Works of Watchman Nee*, vol. 43, pp. 725-726)

Further Reading: The Collected Works of Watchman Nee, vol. 43, ch. 85

Enlightenment and inspiration: _____

_____

_____

_____

_____

Morning Nourishment

Rom. I exhort you therefore, brothers, through the com-
12:1-2 passions of God to present your bodies a living
sacrifice, holy, well pleasing to God, *which is* your
reasonable service. And do not be fashioned according to this age, but be transformed by the renewing
of the mind that you may prove what the will of
God is, that which is good and well pleasing and
perfect.

Today's Reading

Romans 12 speaks in a strong way of the matter of consecration. The consecration there is for service. This service is
a service in the Body of Christ. It is not individual service, but
service in the Body. If a man is not in the Body, it is difficult for
him to understand God's will. I am afraid some people will
misunderstand what we are doing here during the past few
days and will think that we are rallying a fund-raising cam-
paign. If you understand things in this way, you are off. We
have received God's grace to serve Him in this age. In order to
do that, we have to offer up everything and put everything in
the Body. We need to be coordinated in our work and in our
jobs. In order for God to take the fast way, and in order for the
work to reach a high standard, we must have such a kind of
consecration.

Why do we have to touch the matter of riches? It is because
the Lord says, "For where your treasure is, there will your
heart be also" (Matt. 6:21). Where your heart is, there will be
your very person also. Riches are like a nail; they nail a person
down. Perhaps in these few days, some nails have loosened
up. But they have not fallen down yet.

Today, every one of us is still under the tight grip of riches;
they are still nailing us down. May God deliver every one of us
from riches. Romans 12 speaks of two bodies. One is our own
body, and the other is the Body of Christ. We offer up our
bodies for the Body of Christ. If a man has not been delivered

from riches, he cannot offer up his body to God.

Acts 2 and 4 show us that as soon as money goes out, there is the one accord. When the disciples took care of the problem of money, the one accord followed, and God's work was realized in a marvelous way in an instant. The book of Acts is our standard. The first time God saved men, He saved them in great numbers. All those men were delivered from riches. Their service was carried out in the Body. This service in one accord is the Body service spoken of in Romans 12.

If a Christian has not been terminated by God with respect to money, he cannot serve the Lord along with other members. Even if he is to serve, his service will be a superficial one and will not be one that issues from the heart. One of the greatest obstacles to our consecration is the matter of riches. And one of the greatest enemies in the Body of Christ is individualism. In Acts, no one said that anything was his own. If you say that this money is yours, it will be difficult for you to be delivered from individualism. The strongest manifestation of individualism is in the matter of money.

Our way, our work, and our testimony in the future lie with the Body. If the question of money is not settled, we cannot expect to have good coordination, and we cannot expect that we can serve God.

During these years, concerning money, the co-workers can boast that they have not been tied down with jobs for a living. Although the other brothers and sisters have more occasions to be exposed to money, they have to remember that they are serving God just as the co-workers are. We do not expect anyone among us to be a steward for his whole life and yet find nobody to receive him into the eternal tabernacle [Luke 16:9]. (*The Resumption of Watchman Nee's Ministry*, vol. 2, pp. 443-445, 426)

Further Reading: The Resumption of Watchman Nee's Ministry,
    vol. 2, ch. 58

Enlightenment and inspiration: _____

_____

_____

_____

Morning Nourishment

Rom.   For none of us lives to himself, and none dies to
14:7-9   himself; for whether we live, we live to the Lord,
and whether we die, we die to the Lord. Therefore
whether we live or we die, we are the Lord's. For
Christ died and lived *again* for this, that He might
be Lord both of the dead and of the living.

Today's Reading

For one to present his body to God is to go full-time. If you
do not go full-time, how could your body be free to be presented to God as a living sacrifice? Our entire being is con-
tained in our body, and our body is confined in our time.
Therefore, the body is the center of these two things, the
center of our being and the center of our time. The being is
what we are, and the time is where we exist. We can change
the places where we live, but we cannot move ourselves out of
time. You always remain in time. To present your body to God
means you give yourself to God. This is to be full-time. We
Christians should all be full-timers. We have to give ourselves
to Him. We do not give ourselves to anything else, only to our
saving God.

In principle, we have to realize that every saved one should
be a full-timer. This is why Paul has the ground to charge us to
present our bodies to God. Every saved one must be a full-
timer, presenting his body to God....To present your body is
just to present yourself to God. As a saved one, you have to
present yourself to God. Having presented yourself to God,
you will be led by the Lord to either do a job to make money or
to preach the gospel without making any money. Whether
you do a job or preach the gospel depends upon the Lord's
leading.

To be a full-timer means to be one who is absolute for the
Lord. Your income may be five times what you need, yet
you would only spend that one-fifth for your living and give
the other four-fifths to the Lord. To talk about tithing as the

Seventh-Day Adventists practice is a shame. That is something from the Old Testament, something in the law. In the New Testament it is not to present one-tenth but to present your body, to present your entire being. This includes everything you are, everything you have, everything you can do, and everything you earn. It is not just one-tenth but ten-tenths.

The real meaning of being full-time is to live to Him. To go full-time does not mean to drop your job and become a preacher. It does not mean that you give up your business and become one who preaches the gospel or who labors in the word all the time. A full-timer is one who lives to the Lord. Who should be such a one? Every believer, without one exception. As long as you are a believer, you have to realize you should be one living to Him. We have to live to Him because He is ours and we are His. To live to Him is based upon the fact that we are His. Not only is He ours, but we also are His....To live to the Lord includes living for, by, with, and in Him. This is one being two and two in one. There is not only no separation between us and the Lord but also no distinction when we are living to Him.

To be full-time means that you live to the Lord. You do not live for Him but to Him. This is a great privilege. A full-timer does not mean what we may think. A full-timer is one who lives to the Lord; every believer, as one bought by the Lord with a price, should be a person living to the Lord. He is yours and you are His. He and you are one. He is to you and you are to Him. There is no distinction in anything. He does not need your permission to use you, nor do you need His permission to use Him. (*Elders' Training, Book 8: The Life-pulse of the Lord's Present Move*, pp. 105, 111, 113-114, 116-118)

Further Reading: Elders' Training, Book 8: The Life-pulse of the Lord's Present Move, ch. 7

Enlightenment and inspiration: _____ _____

_____

_____

_____

_____

Morning Nourishment

2 Cor. And He died for all that those who live may no
5:15 longer live to themselves but to Him who died for
them and has been raised.

Matt. Who then is the faithful and prudent slave, whom
24:45 the master has set over his household to give them
food at the proper time?

46 Blessed is that slave whom his master, when he
comes, will find so doing.

Today's Reading

I believe we have touched the bottom of the significance of
what it means to be full-time. The job-dropping full-timers
may not have realized that they should be to the Lord. The
most they may have realized is that they are for the Lord.
They are not to the Lord. To be for the Lord means that you
still could be away from the Lord. If you are to the Lord,
you could never be away from Him. To be to the Lord means
that you are one with Him. It means that we breathe to the
Lord, eat to Him, walk to Him, and even exercise to Him. If
you are practicing the real ownership of the Lord, you will do
everything to Him.

I hope we all can realize the proper denotation of the spiritual term *full-time*. To be full-time does not mean that you
need to give up your job. To be a full-timer means that whatever you do, you do to the Lord; whatever you are, you are to
the Lord; and whatever you have, you have to the Lord. If
you remain in a job, you remain there to the Lord. If you leave
your job, you leave it to the Lord. As long as you are to the Lord
you are a full-timer. Whatever you have to do practically all
depends upon the One to whom you live. He leads you. Then
you know whether you have to remain in a job or leave a job or
whether you need to get married or remain single. It does not
mean that if you remain single, you are full-time and that if
you get married, you are not full-time. To be full-time simply
means to live to the Lord.

Every dear saint who really means business with the Lord

must be one all the way living to Him. Paul said that even when we die, we die to Him (Rom. 14:8). Thus, there is no problem concerning whether we live a longer life or whether we die today. If we live, we live to the Lord, and if we die, we die to the Lord. There is no difference. Whatever I do and whatever happens to me, I am to the Lord because I am one with Him. To think that only those who give up their job to do the Lord's work are full-time is a wrong understanding. This is still the understanding under the influence of degraded Christianity....When you say that you are a full-timer, it means that you are to the Lord.

Since October of 1984, I fully realized that we had become somewhat stuck in the Lord's recovery. We held the Lord back very much, so we did not carry out His commission to the recovery....Let us all be full-timers! If we are led to drop our jobs, then we drop them to Him and go out to serve the precious truths....We will gain much increase. Actually, though, I do not care that much for the increase. I care for the spreading of the truths so that they can get into the needy hearts. If we spread these truths, we will become the faithful servants to serve food to the Lord's people at the appointed time (Matt. 24:45). Then we will fulfill the commission of the Lord's recovery. This is where my heart is. I will die to this. I told the brothers in the Far East I will not stop until my entire being is exhausted by this ministry. I hope you all will say the same thing.

Let us rise up to go full-time, either by dropping our jobs to go out or by remaining in our jobs to make more money and give every cent to the Lord's move. Then the Lord's move will not be short of men or money. We will be short of nothing....The wise way is that we all take the full-time way....This is what the Lord needs! (*Elders' Training, Book 8: The Life-pulse of the Lord's Present Move*, pp. 121-123, 126-127)

Further Reading: Elders' Training, Book 8: The Life-pulse of the Lord's Present Move, ch. 8

Enlightenment and inspiration: _____

_____

_____

_____

Hymns, #473

1   No mortal tongue can e'er describe
    The freedom of the soul,
When passed beyond all earthly bribe
    To God's complete control.
All things are his, yes, life, and death,
    Things present or to come;
In Christ he draws in peace each breath,
    In Christ he finds his home.

2   When such as we the King can choose,
    To share with Him His throne,
'Tis passing strange that we refuse
    To be our Lord's alone.
O never speak of sacrifice!
    A privilege untold
Is to be His at any price,
    In Calv'ry's hosts enrolled.

3   Arise! The holy bargain strike—
    The fragment for the whole—
All men and all events alike
    Must serve the ransomed soul.
All things are yours when you are His,
    And He and you are one;
A boundless life in Him there is,
    And kingdom yet to come.

Composition for prophecy with main point and sub-points: _____

_____
_____
_____
_____
_____
_____
_____
_____
_____
_____
_____
_____
_____
_____
_____
_____
_____
_____
_____
_____
_____
_____
_____
_____
_____
_____
_____
_____
_____
_____
_____
_____
_____
_____
_____
_____

Morning Nourishment

Isa. 6:8   Then I heard the voice of the Lord, saying, Whom shall I send? Who will go for us? And I said, Here am I; send me.

Dan.   The people who <u>know</u> their God will <u>show strength</u>
11:32b   and <u>take action</u>.

Today's Reading

Right after [the Gulf War], I reconsidered the world situation. We have to consider what the Lord wants us to do in this present time. <u>There is the need of an appropriate direction for the Lord's move in His recovery today</u> to match the recent <u>changes in the world situation.</u>

The Lord's move and our move are both signified by a wheel. The wheel within the wheel is the Lord's move in our move. When God's people move, God moves. If God's people do not move, God has no way to move.

Recently, a group of brothers traveled to Eastern Europe and Russia, and they have testified of the openness and immense hunger of the people there for the divine truth.

Many of the people in Eastern Europe and Russia will only accept the writings of Watchman Nee and Witness Lee....There is a famine of truth in that part of the world. Some of the people there have even begged the brothers to send people to teach them the Bible.

In both the Far East and the United States, the Lord's recovery is growing, but it is still in the stage of initiation in Europe. <u>We should remember that the United States, Europe, and the Far East are the three influential factors of the present situation of the world.</u> The recovery has taken root in the United States and the Far East, but there is a void in Europe. For this reason, the Lord's direction of His present recovery must be toward Europe. The recovery in Europe is still in the stage of initiation.

The Lord's recovery must spread to Europe and be rooted

there. The spreading of the truths of the Lord's recovery will be a preparation for the Lord's coming back to bring the recovery and restoration not only to Israel but also to the entire creation.

Of the three influential factors in today's world, the Far East and the United States have been occupied and taken by the Lord's recovery. Europe still remains as a region in which the Lord's recovery needs to be rooted and grow. I hope that we would bring this fellowship to the Lord and pray. We should tell the Lord, "Lord, these days are the consummation of the age. Lord, in these days rekindle my love toward You."

The disciples sovereignly were scattered to other places without waiting for the completion of the gospel in the Holy Land [Acts 8:1]. Portions of the Holy Land had not yet heard the gospel, but the Lord was still burdened for the disciples to carry the gospel to other places. Acts 8 also speaks of Philip going to Samaria and eventually preaching the gospel to an Ethiopian eunuch for the spread of the divine truths.

The scattering of the believers from Jerusalem to other localities is the first mentioning of migration for the spreading of the gospel; hence, it should be considered as the basic principle for the spreading of the gospel, including the divine truths. Regardless of whether or not the divine truths have reached the entire United States, we still need to go to Europe. We also have to believe that our going to Europe will stir up something positive in the United States.

To take action [Dan. 11:32] means to do something noble and worthy which may be considered as an achievement. Especially in these days in the Lord's recovery, we need to be those who show strength and take action. (*The World Situation and the Direction of the Lord's Move*, pp. 7, 11, 14, 17, 19, 43-44)

Further Reading: The World Situation and the Direction of the Lord's Move, chs. 1-2

Enlightenment and inspiration: _____

_____

_____

_____

Morning Nourishment

2 Cor. As made sorrowful yet always rejoicing; as poor
6:10 yet enriching many; as having nothing and yet
possessing all things.

Phil. I know also how to be abased, and I know how to
4:12 abound; in everything and in all things I have
learned the secret both to be filled and to hunger,
both to abound and to lack.

Today's Reading

Some need to go to Europe to meet the real need of the
seeking ones with the divine truths from the holy Word.
After the four-day, four-hour war with Iraq, I received a
burden to "invade" Europe with the divine truths of the Lord's
recovery....We should go to Europe by emigration, not by a
work or by a movement. We will be warmly welcomed because
the people there want to receive new things from the West-
ern world. Some of the young people in eastern Berlin begged
the brothers to send people there to teach them the Bible.

Some can emigrate to Europe to live the Lord and serve the
Lord full-time....Some can emigrate there to take a job or do a
business and serve the Lord....Some can emigrate there to
study in a school and serve the Lord.

The full-timers should live a life by faith, trusting in the
Lord for their necessities and receiving the Lord's supply
through the saints and the churches. If we feel led and burdened by the Lord to go full-time, we should not worry about
our necessities. We have to believe in the Lord and put our
trust in Him. We should not think that we will have a prosperous life in material things. We must get ourselves prepared to
suffer. The first suffering is poverty. We need to learn to serve
the Lord in poverty. Some think that if they serve the Lord in
poverty, that is a sign they have not been chosen and called by
the Lord. However, the apostle Paul was in poverty (2 Cor.
6:10; 11:27). Because the churches established by him did not
adequately support him, he was forced to make tents (Acts

18:3). At the same time, he ministered to the needs of his co-workers (20:34).

When I was called by the Lord to serve Him full-time, I thought that He had just called me to preach the gospel to my countrymen in the villages. I told the Lord that as long as I could have water to drink and food to eat, I would be satisfied. I never thought the Lord would bring me to the big cities of mainland China and eventually to Taiwan and the United States. In 1961 I came to the United States with the intention of staying here for the Lord's recovery. At that time I had just a little amount of cash on hand to meet my need. However, the Lord supplied me with enough for my necessities. The Lord is faithful to meet all our needs when we follow Him and His calling.

By the Lord's mercy, I have learned how to be abased in poverty and how to abound (Phil. 4:12). If we have the money, we should learn to save some for others and for the needs of the churches. To serve the Lord in this way is glorious. If the Lord has called us and sent us, He will surely take care of us. He has a way to supply us through the saints and the churches.

When we serve the Lord, we should not have the thought that we are hired in any sense by anyone or by any church. If the church supplies us, that does not mean that the church hires us. That is not a wage but the Lord's supply through the church. We have to fully realize that the Lord in supporting us needs His Body (the church) and the members of His Body (the believers) to cooperate with Him. He does not supply us directly by Himself but indirectly through His Body and His members. (*The World Situation and the Direction of the Lord's Move*, pp. 45-47, 54-56)

Further Reading: The World Situation and the Direction of the Lord's Move, chs. 3-4

Enlightenment and inspiration: _____

_____

_____

_____

_____

Morning Nourishment

2 Cor. But *it is* out of equality; at the present time your
8:14 abundance for their lack that their abundance
      also may be for your lack, so that there may be
      equality;
  15 As it is written, "He who *gathered* much had no
      excess, and he who *gathered* little had no lack."

Today's Reading

In 2 Corinthians 8:12-15 Paul says we must give willingly
according to what we have. Those who gathered much will
have no excess, and those who gathered little will have no
lack. The result of such giving and receiving is what Paul calls
"equality" (v. 14). Equality equals having everything common,
but there are different means of practicing this.

We must remember that God's principle is to have equality.
Even in the Old Testament there is the divine way to balance
the social wealth. None of the Jews could sell their property
forever....In the year of jubilee everything was returned to the
original owner (Lev. 25:8-17). God's way is to keep equality.

The Bible encourages us to support the full-time workers.
Third John 5-8 tells us we need to take care of, support, and
send the traveling full-time workers forward on their way in a
way that matches God, who is generous. If we support the
full-timers, we are participating, sharing, in their work for the
truth, and we become "fellow workers in the truth" (v. 8). We
are not directly taking part of the full-time work, but we are
indirectly sharing the same work. The believers ought to support and undertake for the need of the brothers who work for
God in His divine truth and who take nothing from the Gentiles. Therefore, if you do not have the burden to be full-time,
you should make more money for the Lord's interest. Do not
work merely to support yourself, but also to support the full-
time workers. Even the wives whose husbands are full-time
workers could work to support their husbands and other
full-timers if possible. This will be greatly blessed by the Lord.

(*The Way to Practice the Lord's Present Move,* pp. 71-73)

The full-timers who would still remain in their job, their profession or business, to make money...remain there to make a gain of the world's gold. When the Israelites left Egypt, they plundered it of its gold (Exo. 11:2-3; 12:35-36). The material gold mine is in Egypt. We need some full-timers to remain there to dig the gold mine to get the gold. The other full-timers will drop their job, profession, or business for the preaching and teaching of the gospel truth, but they will need something to live on. We would not like to see that they would be forced to make tents as Paul was in Acts 18:1-3. That would be a shame to us. If I were there at Paul's time, I would have gone through all the churches to tell them that it was a shame that they would not have fellowship with the apostle Paul unto the gospel (Phil. 1:5). It was a shame to force him and his co-workers to go back to "Egypt" to get some gold. We must stress to the saints that we are all full-timers in different functions. Some have the function to preach the gospel, teach the truth, and minister life to all the seekers. However, these dear ones could not have any time to make a living. They need others to support them. Therefore, a great number of us full-timers should remain in our jobs, professions, or businesses to make money.

It is a great thing to have fellowship unto the gospel. Unto the gospel means for the furtherance of the gospel. All the full-timers who remain in their jobs and businesses need to have this kind of fellowship, a fellowship for the furtherance of the Lord's move through those who do not remain in businesses and jobs, but who are occupied all day with preaching and teaching for the spreading of the Lord's kingdom. (*Elders' Training, Book 8: The Life-pulse of the Lord's Present Move,* pp. 129-130)

Further Reading: The Way to Practice the Lord's Present Move, ch. 5

Enlightenment and inspiration: _____

_____

_____

_____

Morning Nourishment

Acts And all those who believed were together and had
2:44 all things common.
4:32 And the heart and soul of the multitude of those
who had believed was one; and not even one said
that any of his possessions was his own, but all
things were common to them.

Today's Reading

It is not sufficient to use the Seventh-Day Adventists as an example, reminding the saints how they practice ten percent tithing. This is too poor. The tithing of ten percent to the Lord is altogether an Old Testament thing, belonging to the law. There was no grace, life, or life power in that. We must be different. We are in the age of grace, which provides us with much supply of life. The dynamic salvation was accepted by Zaccheus in Luke 19:1-10. Immediately after being saved, that sinner gave up so much of his worldly possessions. That was not a tithing of ten percent; that was the very issue of the dynamic salvation. Likewise, on the day of Pentecost all those small members had everything in common (Acts 2:44, 45; 4:32-35). This was not one tenth of their possessions but one hundred percent. They put everything at the feet of the apostles, that is, at the Lord's disposal. That was wonderful. We are in the Lord's recovery; even this matter has to be recovered.

Train the saints who love the Lord so much. It is regrettable that in the past they did not receive the adequate education or instruction in this matter. The more they would spend for the Lord, the more they have the blessing spoken of in Philippians 4:19. Give this verse to all the dear ones who love the Lord and are full-time to make money and to give. This verse is a great blessing. Quite often when I receive a gift from a dear saint, I quote this verse as a conclusion to my letter of acknowledgment: "My God will fill your every need according to His riches, in glory, in Christ Jesus." Because you are taking

care of God's need, God would give you a great blessing in fill-
ing every need of yours according to His riches. I have seen in
the past that those who did care for God's need all received a
bountiful blessing. The saints' giving will not be in vain. The
more they give, the more they will see the Lord's riches. Due to
the good government, the good administration in Taiwan, the
people there have become rich. We have to give the credit to
our sovereign God. Now all the saints there in Taiwan can
share the riches. We have to pray that God would keep blessing the United States for His purpose. The Lord's recovery
needs much blessing that comes from God's sovereignty through
the government. The recovery needs the United States as its
center.

Train the saints in your locality. Do not merely enjoy the
physical gains you have received under God's sovereignty.
This may offend the Lord. In this case the Lord will take
back His blessing. Train the saints to realize that if we are
faithful to Him, He will bless us. If we spend every ounce of
our gold for His purpose, He will return to us not only by
ounces, but by pounds. This is to carry out the fellowship
unto the gospel, the fellowship for the furtherance of the
gospel.

The key point of this way is that every believer is a full-
timer. Some drop their job to preach and teach, while some
remain on their job to make money. We must encourage
some to drop their jobs. We must also encourage some to
make money and separate five percent monthly, purposely
for the account of the fellowship unto the gospel. (*Elders'
Training, Book 8: The Life-pulse of the Lord's Present Move*,
pp. 130-132, 137)

*Further Reading: Elders' Training, Book 8: The Life-pulse of the
Lord's Present Move, ch. 9*

Enlightenment and inspiration: _____

_____

_____

_____

_____

_____

Morning Nourishment

Phil. And you yourselves also know, Philippians, that in
4:15-16 the beginning of the gospel, when I went out from
Macedonia, no church had fellowship with me in
the account of giving and receiving except you
only; for even in Thessalonica you sent both once
and again to my need.

19 And my God will fill your every need according to
His riches, in glory, in Christ Jesus.

Today's Reading

What kind of sweet feeling the apostle expressed [in
Philippians 4:15-16]! He said this was "a sweet-smelling savor,
an acceptable sacrifice, well-pleasing to God" (v. 18). Paul did
not seek a gift from them (v. 17), but what they gave became a
sweet savor for Paul to put on the altar for them. It was not
merely something to support him, but it became something
increasing to their account. There is an account in the heavenly
bank, in which we may have credit or debit. It is merely a low
practice to give ten percent. God is not a beggar; do not treat
Him as one. You should honor Him as the very bountiful Giver
who affords you all the riches. All your riches come from Him. It
was and still is up to Him whether you will be rich or not. It is
not according to your plan of what you should do and have. You
simply must labor day and night. He then will follow your labor
to bless you, not for your enterprise, but for the spreading of
His kingdom.

In any church out of twenty there must be one who drops his
business or profession to take the full-time way to preach and
to teach. The nineteen others should do their best regularly,
even weekly, to put aside a certain amount of their monthly
income for the supporting of such a one. For nineteen to support one would be, humanly speaking, very easy. Each one
simply saves five percent of their income. This would be sufficient to support the one who drops his job. This ninety-five percent is the equivalent of a full-time job for the one who drops his

job. This will not burden the church. It will be easy.

Charge the dear saints that besides their regular giving to the Lord through the church, they should give an additional five percent of their income every month. Do not do it once a year. It is better to...put one portion every Lord's Day into the offering box.

Whether or not in your locality there are these job-dropping full-timers, you should still practice this. In your place there may not be such, yet in other places there may be....They should practice to save five percent of their income to take care of those in the other halls, in other churches, and even in other countries. If we are in one accord on the whole earth, the church must practice this, encouraging and charging all the saints each month to designate five percent of their income specifically for supporting the job-dropping full-timers throughout the whole earth.

Do not say that you do not have any job-dropping full-timers. All the churches on the earth have to do this. Leave to the Lord how much will be accomplished, but you must practice the five percent giving. Train everyone among us to practice the putting aside of an extra five percent, putting it aside uniquely for the fellowship unto the gospel. I believe that the Lord will bless this. This is for His spreading. How much He desires to spread through us! But for this spreading today, there is the need of financial support. We do not need to have a fund raising movement. We do not need to send someone to convince all the churches to contribute money. We simply need a regular, weekly practice of giving in this way, designated for the fellowship unto the gospel....Every church should have such a separate "Fellowship unto the Gospel" account. (*Elders' Training, Book 8: The Life-pulse of the Lord's Present Move,* pp. 134, 136-137)

Further Reading: Elders' Training, Book 8: The Life-pulse of the Lord's Present Move, ch. 9

Enlightenment and inspiration: _____

_____

_____

_____

Morning Nourishment

1 Cor. On the first day of the week each one of you should
16:2   lay aside in store to himself whatever he may have
        been prospered, that no collections be made when
        I come.

Today's Reading

If we mean business with the Lord for the spreading of all
the truths He has shown us, we all have to bear the burden
to give five percent of our income purely, solely, and definitely
separate for the full-time workers' support. Every time you
give to the Lord through the church, five percent of your income
should be given to the Lord to support full-time workers for His
propagation. Every church that has at least twenty members
should practice this. A church smaller than twenty may still
have one or two among them who are burdened to be full-time.
Suppose a church can only support one full-timer, but two
among them are burdened and qualified to be full-time. One of
these two should not be told to go back and get a job. Some
churches may have twenty members with no full-time workers. Then their five percent can be given to a church that has an
extra number of full-time workers. This is done not by organi-
zation but by fellowship.

I hope all the churches will begin to practice this regardless
of whether or not they have full-time workers and regardless of
how many workers they have. The leading ones should fellowship with the saints concerning giving five percent of their
income for the full-time workers. Then the church should set up
a separate account for the support of full-timers whether it has
a full-timer or not. The funds in this account will eventually be
useful. The Lord desires many full-time workers for His present move. Within 1986 I expect that all the churches in the
United States would have between four and five hundred
full-time workers.

If a church of one hundred saints only has three full-
time workers, they should have an extra supply for two other

full-time workers. Through fellowship with the other churches, they will be able to realize where there are places with full-time workers who need support. We all need to pray and seek the Lord's leading regarding this matter. There should only be a principle set up with no regulation. The church needs to take care of the principle of setting aside five percent of the offerings for the full-time workers. But this does not exclude the saints from giving to the full-timers directly. (*The Way to Practice the Lord's Present Move*, pp. 75-76)

According to the Bible, the offerings made by the believers in the meetings should be used for: (1) the local expenses, for example, rent, etc., (2) the relief of the brothers and sisters who are in poverty and want, and (3) the assistance of the workers and the expenses for the work, as commanded by the Bible. Actually, the workers of a locality should be supported by the believers of that locality. The funds of the meetings should be used in such a manner. The individual believer still has a responsibility towards relieving the poor and assisting the workers and the work.

Now we have two offering boxes, and each box has two partitions. There are two openings on the top of each box. The funds for the church meetings should be put into one opening, and the funds for the work should be put into the other opening. This is necessary because, in the past, some have put funds meant for the work into the box for the meetings. In this way the meetings have taken advantage of the work....If there is money designated for an individual worker, it should be wrapped up in paper with the name of the worker written on it. Although the boxes are there, the surplus or deficit of the funds for the work is the responsibility of the workers; they are not the responsibility of the brothers and sisters in the meetings. (*The Collected Works of Watchman Nee*, vol. 17, pp. 214-215)

Further Reading: The Way to Practice the Lord's Present Move,
    ch. 5

Enlightenment and inspiration: _____

_____

_____

_____

Hymns, #445

1 Take my life, and let it be
Consecrated, Lord, to Thee;
Take my moments and my days,
Let them flow in ceaseless praise.

2 Take my hands, and let them move
At the impulse of Thy love;
Take my feet and let them be
Swift and beautiful for Thee.

3 Take my voice, and let me sing
Always, only, for my King;
Take my lips, and let them be
Filled with messages from Thee.

4 Take my silver and my gold;
Not a mite would I withhold;
Take my intellect, and use
Every power as Thou shalt choose.

5 Take my will, and make it Thine;
It shall be no longer mine.
Take my heart; it is Thine own;
It shall be Thy royal throne.

6 Take my love; my Lord, I pour
At Thy feet its treasure-store.
Take myself, and I will be
Ever, only, all for Thee.

*Composition for prophecy with main point and
sub-points:* _____

Morning Nourishment

2 Cor.
8:7

But just as you abound in everything, in faith and in word and in knowledge and in all earnestness and in the love in you from us, abound in this grace also.

13-15

For *it is* not that to others *there would be* relief, *yet* to you affliction, but *it is* out of equality; at the present time your abundance for their lack that their abundance also may be for your lack, so that there may be equality; as it is written, "He who *gathered* much had no excess, and he who *gathered* little had no lack."

Today's Reading

In the wilderness the children of Israel did not do any farming, sowing, or reaping. Instead, they gathered manna. Some may have been greedy and tried to gather a large amount of manna, much more than they needed. However, by the end of the day, what was left was no longer useful....In the case of those who gathered an excess of manna, perhaps wanting to store it up for days and weeks to come, God caused the excess to be taken away.

Those who were rather feeble and not able to gather much manna did not have any lack. The divine way is that those who gathered little had no lack and those who gathered much had nothing over. This is God's heavenly way of balancing the supply among His people....God balances the daily supply among His children by His sovereign and miraculous hand.

In 2 Corinthians 8 Paul likens our giving to the needy ones to the gathering of manna. To our realization, we are giving, not gathering. But what Paul says indicates that our giving is a gathering. Paul's word at least implies that as children of God we should not be greedy. We should not think that if we earn a large sum of money, we shall be able to preserve it all for ourselves. We need to see that whether we give or not, eventually the outcome will be the same.

Suppose a brother earns $40,000 a year, but what he actually needs for his living is much less than that amount. Being rather greedy, he wants to reserve a large amount for himself. He tithes ten percent, or $4000, with the intention of keeping the other $36,000. This tithing is a good practice. However, it is possible for this brother to follow an even better way. According to this better way, the brother should keep what he needs for his living, perhaps $20,000, and give away the remainder. No doubt, humanly speaking, almost everyone would follow the first way, the way of tithing, instead of the second way, the way of giving all that he can. If the brother decides to tithe and keep the extra $16,000 for himself, eventually he will learn that, in His sovereignty, God has many ways to cause this excess money to disappear. There may be illness, accident, or calamity. If the money does not disappear in this generation, it will disappear in the following generation or certainly in the third generation. God's mighty, sovereign hand will be active to practice a heavenly balancing of the wealth among His people.

No matter how wise you may be in the handling of money, God is wiser. As the heavenly pilot, he knows how to cause your money to fly away. He did this with the manna in the Old Testament, and does it with money today. The question that faces you is this: do you want to balance the material supply willingly, or will you force God to balance it in a miraculous, sovereign way? I can assure you that sooner or later you will be balanced in financial matters. Concerning this, we need to understand God's heart. Deep in His heart God desires that His people be balanced in the daily supply....You should remember that whether or not you willingly share with others, eventually the outcome will be the same. *(Life-study of 2 Corinthians,* pp. 419-422)

Further Reading: Life-study of 2 Corinthians, msg. 48

Enlightenment and inspiration: _____

_____

_____

_____

Morning Nourishment

2 Cor. But *take note of* this: He who sows sparingly shall
9:6-7 also sparingly reap; and he who sows with blessings shall also with blessings reap; each one as he
has purposed in his heart, not out of sorrow or out
of necessity, for God loves a cheerful giver.

Prov. There is one who scatters and increases yet more, /
11:24 And there is one who withholds what is appropriate, *but ends up* only in want.

Today's Reading

The Christian way of managing money is not to hold on to
money. The tighter you hold on to your money, the more it dies.
The more you grasp it, the more it disappears; it will evapo-
rate like vapor. But the more you give away, the more you will
have. If God's children would learn to give more, God would
have many ways to work out His miracles. Keeping back
money only makes God's children poor. God will not entrust
Himself to those who hold on to their money and who will not
give. The more you give, the more God will give to you.

Please read 2 Corinthians 9:6, which says, "He who sows
sparingly shall also sparingly reap; and he who sows with
blessings shall also with blessings reap." This is also a scrip-
tural principle of financial management. When Christians
give, they are not throwing their money away; they are
sowing. The Word does not say, "He who throws away his
money sparingly shall also sparingly reap; and he who throws
away his money with blessings shall also with blessings reap."
It says, "He who sows sparingly shall also sparingly reap;
and he who sows with blessings shall also with blessings
reap." When you give, you are sowing. Do you want your
money to grow? If you do, you need to sow. When you give
your money away, it grows. When you do not give it away, it
does not grow.

Brothers and sisters, can anyone be so foolish as to expect
a harvest without sowing? How many times has God not

answered your prayer for your needs? You are a "hard man," trying to reap where you have not sown and gather where you have not winnowed. This is impossible. Why do you not sow some of your money? There are many brothers and sisters who are in difficulty. Why do you not sow money upon them so that you may reap when the reaping time comes? The more a person holds on to his money, the less he will have. In the above portion of the Word, we see a very beautiful picture. The Corinthians gave to those in Jerusalem, remembering their needs, and Paul said that it was a kind of sowing, not a kind of throwing away. Please remember that money can be our seeds. If you see a brother or sister in difficulty, and you remember him or her, God will cause that money to grow and harvest thirtyfold, sixtyfold, and even a hundredfold. I hope that more of your money will be sown.

A new believer should learn to sow, so that when he has needs, he can reap what he has sown. You cannot reap what you have not sown. There are many brothers who are getting poorer and poorer. If you eat what you have, of course, there will not be anything left. But if you keep half of your seed for sowing, you will have a harvest next year. If next year you also keep half for planting, you will have another harvest the following year. If you want to sow anything, you must not eat all that you have. Some people always eat and never sow. They also never receive anything when they are in need. Suppose some young brothers sow some money upon other brothers, praying as they sow, "O God, I have sown upon the brothers. When I have needs, I want to harvest." If they do this, God will honor His own words. (*The Collected Works of Watchman Nee,* vol. 49, pp. 429-431)

Further Reading: The Collected Works of Watchman Nee, vol. 49, ch. 28

Enlightenment and inspiration: _____

_____

_____

_____

_____

Morning Nourishment

2 Cor. Now He who bountifully supplies seed to the sower
9:10-11 and bread for food will supply and multiply your
seed and cause the fruits of your righteousness to
increase. You in everything are being enriched
unto all liberality, which works out through us
thanksgiving to God.

Today's Reading

[Second Corinthians 9:6 speaks of] a natural law established by the Lord in the biological realm. This law contains
His promise. Offering material riches is like sowing. Since
sowing eventually brings in reaping, he who sows sparingly
shall reap sparingly, and he who sows bountifully shall reap
bountifully. In man's eyes, the offering of material riches is
to give away their riches. However, in God's eyes, such offering
is a kind of sowing which will result in reaping. He...who
offers much shall reap much. We ought to believe in the Lord's
promise in this law. (Life Lessons, p. 182)

According to 9:6, he who sows sparingly shall also reap
sparingly, and he who sows with blessings shall also reap with
blessings. In verse 6 we have the thought of sowing for the
benefit of others. But what farmer, when he sows seed in his
field, has the thought of sowing for others? Surely, most farm-
ers have the concept of sowing for themselves. This kind of
sowing, however, is not with blessings. To sow with blessings
is to give to others....When we give of our money, we are
sowing, and this sowing is not for ourselves, but is for others.
If we sow with blessings to others, we shall reap with blessings from God.

When we sow with blessings to others, we shall reap with
blessings from God. Furthermore, the harvest will always
far surpass the amount of seed sown. It may be multiplied
thirty or even one hundred times. This does not happen
miraculously; it takes place according to natural law. God con-
trols the life supply among His children by miracles. Because

of this, no Christian family can maintain its wealth for generations. But sowing is according to natural law, not according to miracle. Regarding this, there is no need for God to do anything miraculous. We all need to sow, to give. The more we give, the more we shall reap. However, we should not do this in a superstitious way for the purpose of gaining riches for ourselves.

The two illustrations of gathering and sowing are related to Paul's profound thoughts in these chapters. In chapter nine the deep thought is that as Christians we give in the sense of sowing. Moreover, we should not sow sparingly. If we sow sparingly, then according to natural law we shall reap sparingly. We need to sow with blessings to others. If we sow with blessings to others, then, also according to natural law, we shall reap with blessings from God to us. This blessing will be many times more than what we have sown....The Lord will always honor the natural law He has ordained.

We should sow more and in turn reap more. The goal is not to make ourselves rich. The result is the abounding of thanksgiving to God [9:11]. I hope that in the time to come many of the saints will become a factor of thanksgiving to God. This means that your giving will abound in much thanksgiving to God. I have the full confidence that if the saints in the Lord's recovery are willing to give, the recovery will never be lacking in material supply. Instead of lack, there will be abounding in thanksgiving to the Lord through many saints. Therefore, let us all practice our giving, a giving which is carried out by gathering and by sowing. (*Life-study of 2 Corinthians*, pp. 422, 425-426)

Further Reading: Life-study of 2 Corinthians, msgs. 48-49

Enlightenment and inspiration: _____

_____

_____

_____

_____

_____

_____

Morning Nourishment

Matt.   Do not store up for yourselves treasures on the
6:19-21 earth, where moth and rust consume and where
        thieves dig through and steal. But store up for your-
        selves treasures in heaven, where neither moth
        nor rust consumes and where thieves do not dig
        through nor steal. For where your treasure is,
        there will your heart be also.
31-33   Therefore do not be anxious, saying, What shall we
        eat? or, What shall we drink? or, With what shall
        we be clothed? For all these things the Gentiles are
        anxiously seeking. For your heavenly Father knows
        that you need all these things. But seek first His
        kingdom and His righteousness, and all these things
        will be added to you.

Today's Reading

In [Matthew 6:19-20] the King decrees that the kingdom
people should not lay up for themselves treasures on earth,
but treasures in heaven. To lay up treasures in heaven is to
give material things to the poor (19:21) and to care for the
needy saints (Acts 2:45; 4:34-35; 11:29; Rom. 15:26) and for
the Lord's servants (Phil. 4:16-17). Verse 21 says, "For where
your treasure is, there will your heart be also." The kingdom
people must send their treasure to heaven so that their heart
can also be in heaven. Before they go there, their treasure and
their heart must go there first.

Apparently, in this section...the Lord is speaking about the
dealing of the kingdom people with material riches. Actually,
He is dealing with the matter of anxiety....It may also seem
that the Lord is touching our heart, for where our treasure is,
there our heart is also....The whole world is involved with
anxiety. Anxiety is the gear that makes the world move. It is
the incentive for all human culture. If there were no anxiety
regarding our living, no one would do anything. Rather, everyone would be idle. Thus, by touching our anxiety, the Lord

touches the gear of human life.

Let us now consider the Lord's intention in verses 19 through 34. Does the Lord intend that the young people finish school, or drop out and be like birds in the air? It is wrong to have anxiety, for anxiety does not belong to the divine life. There is no anxiety in the life of God. However, the Lord does not mean that we should not do our duty. When the Lord brought the children of Israel into the good land, they all had to work on the land. That was their duty....They labored not only for themselves, but also for the birds. If they did not do the work of farming, it would have been difficult for the birds to live. To do their duty was right and necessary, but to have anxiety was wrong. Likewise, we must do our duty today, but do it without being anxious about our living. The reason you are so reluctant to give to others is your anxiety. Because of anxiety, you love the material things. If you had no anxiety, you would not care for the material things. Rather, you would let others have them. It is anxiety that causes us trouble.

After a number of years, many of our young people will have college degrees. I believe that under the Lord's sovereign blessing, many riches will come in. At that time you will need to remember that you have gone to school not for anxiety, but to do your duty. Therefore, the riches that you bring in should not be used for your anxiety, but for your duty. Your duty is to give, to lay up treasures in heaven. Do not aspire to be a millionaire. Do not endeavor to have a savings account of a million dollars. Rather, learn to give and lay up treasures in heaven. Transfer your treasures from the earth to the heavens. In this way you will not be a millionaire on earth, but a millionaire in the heavens....Be a good giver according to the life and nature of your heavenly Father. (*Life-study of Matthew*, pp. 271, 273, 275-279)

Further Reading: Life-study of Matthew, msg. 22

Enlightenment and inspiration: _____

_____

_____

_____

Morning Nourishment

1 Tim.   Charge those who are rich in the present age not
6:17-19 to be high-minded, nor to set their hope on the
         uncertainty of riches but on God, who affords us
         all things richly for *our* enjoyment; to do good, to
         be rich in good works, to be ready to distribute, to
         be ones willing to share; laying away for them-
         selves a good foundation as a treasure for the
         future, that they may lay hold on that which is
         really life.

Today's Reading

From the time that man developed a problem with God because of the fall and left the position where he took God as everything, material riches have become a critical matter in the life of fallen man. In his fallen condition, man fell into the darkness of acknowledging only material riches and not God, of trusting only in material riches and not in God, and even of serving material riches, taking material riches as God, and allowing material riches to replace God. God's enemy, Satan the devil, exploited the fallen condition of men to come in and deceive men to worship idols, such as the god of wealth, for riches and gain. By being behind these idols, he supplants men's worship and service that are due God. For this reason, the Lord Jesus told us that one "cannot serve God and mammon" (Matt. 6:24). Literally, the service spoken of by the Lord here refers to the service of a slave....This tells us that Satan utilizes material riches to seduce people to worship him on the one hand, and enslaves people in material riches, as misers, on the other hand. However, we have received God's mercy and the Lord's salvation, which delivered us from the authority of Satan and turned us to God (Acts 26:18). After we have received God's salvation in this way, we are confronted with an issue in our practical living, that is, what should we do with material riches that Satan used in time past to delude us and all the world....Should we be the same as we were in the old manner of living before we were saved? Or should we have a change regarding our material riches according to the salvation which delivered us from the authority of Satan and turned us to God?

[First Timothy 6:17] exposes Satan's plot to delude men, showing us that all the material things and enjoyment in our living apparently come from the uncertain riches, but they actually come from God's giving. They are supplied to us from God's rich giving. Hence, we must not set our hope on deceitful and uncertain material riches, but on the very God who gives us all things richly for our enjoyment.

We ought to endeavor in our businesses. The Bible also requires that we learn to maintain good works for necessary needs (Titus 3:14, 8). Yet without God's blessing, all our labors, endeavorings, and painstaking enterprises will yield little. Therefore, in this matter of material supply, unlike the worldly people who trust only in their own abilities, we have to learn to set our hope in God.

[First Timothy 6:17-19] is the apostle's charge, which is simply the Lord's charge to us. The rich refers to those who have excess from their gain after the needs of their living have been met. To do good and to be rich in good works refer to distributing the surplus from one's living to the needy ones. To be rich in doing good and good works is to be ready to distribute and willing to communicate. This is also to lay up treasure in heaven, to lay up as a treasure a good foundation for the future. Doing this will enable one to lay hold on, that is, to possess, to use, and to enjoy, that which is really life, the eternal life of God. To save up the surplus riches from our living on the earth is to lay hold on and make use of our natural life; while to save up the same in heaven, spending it on God, is to lay hold on and employ the eternal life of God. (*Life Lessons,* pp. 179-181)

Further Reading: Life Lessons, lsn. 24

Enlightenment and inspiration: _____

_____

_____

Morning Nourishment

1 Cor.   Now concerning the collection for the saints, just
16:1-2   as I directed the churches of Galatia, so you also
         do. On the first day of the week each one of you
         should lay aside in store to himself whatever he
         may have been prospered, that no collections be
         made when I come.

Today's Reading

All of fallen mankind are under the domination of mammon and material possessions (Matt. 6:19-21, 24-25, 30; 19:21-22; Luke 12:13-19). At the day of Pentecost, under the power of the Holy Spirit, all the believers overthrew this domination and had all their possessions in common for distribution to the needy ones (Acts 2:44-45; 4:32, 34-37). That practice, due to the weakness of the believers' fallen nature (see Acts 5:1-11; 6:1), did not last long. It was already over by the apostle Paul's time. Then the believers needed grace to overcome the power of mammon and material things and to release them from Satan's domination for an offering to the Lord to fulfill His purpose. Resurrection life is the supply for the believers to live such a life, a life trusting in God, not in treasures of material possessions, a life not for today but for the future, not for this age but for the coming age (Luke 12:16-21; 1 Tim. 6:17-19), a life that overthrows the usurpation of temporal and uncertain riches....This dealing is related to God's administration among the churches.

It is a crucial matter that this dealing follows a chapter concerning the reality of resurrection life. Resurrection is not only the power over sin and death; resurrection is a power over mammon and material possessions. Therefore, immediately following the chapter on resurrection, Paul turns to the matter of material possessions.

In the second section of 1 Corinthians, chapters eleven through sixteen, Paul deals with matters in the realm of the divine administration. This section begins with the headship of God and consummates with a seemingly insignificant matter—the gift of material things for the saints. Whether or not we are truly in God's administration...and are carrying out God's administration, can be tested by how we are related to material things and how we handle our money. If we use our money in a worldly way, then no matter what we say about resurrection, we are not truly in God's administration. The extent to which we are in the divine administration...is determined by how we care for money and material possessions.

If we all would be faithful to live for God's administration in caring for money and material matters, there would be no financial needs in the recovery. For example, certainly we can exercise our spirit and our will to save a small amount of money each week, perhaps just two dollars and fifty cents, and give this to the Lord for His move on the earth. One day, instead of having our lunch at a restaurant, we may eat a simple meal prepared at home. Then the money saved could be given to the Lord. Imagine what the situation would be if we all were faithful to do something like this week by week!

In such a spiritual book dealing with spiritual and heavenly matters, Paul eventually turns to the very practical matter of finances. It is quite easy to talk about the headship and say, "Praise the Lord, I am under the headship of Christ! Christ is my Head. Concerning His headship, I do not have any problems." But can you say that you have no problem with the matter Paul brings up in chapter sixteen? We may talk about the victory of resurrection over sin and death, but what about the victory in resurrection over your use of your money and material possessions?...For this reason, Paul, in God's wisdom, deals with the matter of giving immediately after the matter of resurrection. (*Life-study of 1 Corinthians*, pp. 625-628)

Further Reading: Life-study of 1 Corinthians, msg. 69, pp. 625-628

Enlightenment and inspiration: _____

_____

_____

_____

Hymns, #433

1   I am the Lord's! O joy beyond expression,
        O sweet response to voice of love Divine;
    Faith's joyous "Yes" to the assuring whisper,
        "Fear not! I have redeemed thee; thou art Mine."

2   I am the Lord's! It is the glad confession
        Wherewith the Bride recalls the happy day,
    When love's "I will" accepted Him forever,
        "The Lord's," to love, to honor and obey.

3   I am the Lord's! Yet teach me all it meaneth,
        All it involves of love and loyalty,
    Of holy service, absolute surrender,
        And unreserved obedience unto Thee.

4   I am the Lord's! Yes; body, soul, and spirit,
        O seal them irrecoverably Thine;
    As Thou, Beloved, in Thy grace and fulness
        Forever and forevermore art mine.

*Composition for prophecy with main point and
sub-points:* _____

_____

_____

_____

_____

_____

_____

_____

_____

_____

_____

_____

_____

_____

_____

_____

_____

_____

_____

_____

_____

_____

_____

_____

_____

_____

_____

_____

_____

_____

_____

_____

_____

_____

Reading Schedule for the Recovery Version of the Old Testament with Footnotes

Wk.	Lord's Day	Monday	Tuesday	Wednesday	Thursday	Friday	Saturday
1	Gen. 1:1-5 ☐	1:6-23 ☐	1:24-31 ☐	2:1-9 ☐	2:10-25 ☐	3:1-13 ☐	3:14-24 ☐
2	4:1-26 ☐	5:1-32 ☐	6:1-22 ☐	7:1—8:3 ☐	8:4-22 ☐	9:1-29 ☐	10:1-32 ☐
3	11:1-32 ☐	12:1-20 ☐	13:1-18 ☐	14:1-24 ☐	15:1-21 ☐	16:1-16 ☐	17:1-27 ☐
4	18:1-33 ☐	19:1-38 ☐	20:1-18 ☐	21:1-34 ☐	22:1-24 ☐	23:1—24:27 ☐	24:28-67 ☐
5	25:1-34 ☐	26:1-35 ☐	27:1-46 ☐	28:1-22 ☐	29:1-35 ☐	30:1-43 ☐	31:1-55 ☐
6	32:1-32 ☐	33:1—34:31 ☐	35:1-29 ☐	36:1-43 ☐	37:1-36 ☐	38:1—39:23 ☐	40:1—41:13 ☐
7	41:14-57 ☐	42:1-38 ☐	43:1-34 ☐	44:1-34 ☐	45:1-28 ☐	46:1-34 ☐	47:1-31 ☐
8	48:1-22 ☐	49:1-15 ☐	49:16-33 ☐	50:1-26 ☐	Exo. 1:1-22 ☐	2:1-25 ☐	3:1-22 ☐
9	4:1-31 ☐	5:1-23 ☐	6:1-30 ☐	7:1-25 ☐	8:1-32 ☐	9:1-35 ☐	10:1-29 ☐
10	11:1-10 ☐	12:1-14 ☐	12:15-36 ☐	12:37-51 ☐	13:1-22 ☐	14:1-31 ☐	15:1-27 ☐
11	16:1-36 ☐	17:1-16 ☐	18:1-27 ☐	19:1-25 ☐	20:1-26 ☐	21:1-36 ☐	22:1-31 ☐
12	23:1-33 ☐	24:1-18 ☐	25:1-22 ☐	25:23-40 ☐	26:1-14 ☐	26:15-37 ☐	27:1-21 ☐
13	28:1-21 ☐	28:22-43 ☐	29:1-21 ☐	29:22-46 ☐	30:1-10 ☐	30:11-38 ☐	31:1-17 ☐
14	31:18—32:35 ☐	33:1-23 ☐	34:1-35 ☐	35:1-35 ☐	36:1-38 ☐	37:1-29 ☐	38:1-31 ☐
15	39:1-43 ☐	40:1-38 ☐	Lev. 1:1-17 ☐	2:1-16 ☐	3:1-17 ☐	4:1-35 ☐	5:1-19 ☐
16	6:1-30 ☐	7:1-38 ☐	8:1-36 ☐	9:1-24 ☐	10:1-20 ☐	11:1-47 ☐	12:1-8 ☐
17	13:1-28 ☐	13:29-59 ☐	14:1-18 ☐	14:19-32 ☐	14:33-57 ☐	15:1-33 ☐	16:1-17 ☐
18	16:18-34 ☐	17:1-16 ☐	18:1-30 ☐	19:1-37 ☐	20:1-27 ☐	21:1-24 ☐	22:1-33 ☐
19	23:1-22 ☐	23:23-44 ☐	24:1-23 ☐	25:1-23 ☐	25:24-55 ☐	26:1-24 ☐	26:25-46 ☐
20	27:1-34 ☐	Num. 1:1-54 ☐	2:1-34 ☐	3:1-51 ☐	4:1-49 ☐	5:1-31 ☐	6:1-27 ☐
21	7:1-41 ☐	7:42-88 ☐	7:89—8:26 ☐	9:1-23 ☐	10:1-36 ☐	11:1-35 ☐	12:1—13:33 ☐
22	14:1-45 ☐	15:1-41 ☐	16:1-50 ☐	17:1—18:7 ☐	18:8-32 ☐	19:1-22 ☐	20:1-29 ☐
23	21:1-35 ☐	22:1-41 ☐	23:1-30 ☐	24:1-25 ☐	25:1-18 ☐	26:1-65 ☐	27:1-23 ☐
24	28:1-31 ☐	29:1-40 ☐	30:1—31:24 ☐	31:25-54 ☐	32:1-42 ☐	33:1-56 ☐	34:1-29 ☐
25	35:1-34 ☐	36:1-13 ☐	Deut. 1:1-46 ☐	2:1-37 ☐	3:1-29 ☐	4:1-49 ☐	5:1-33 ☐
26	6:1—7:26 ☐	8:1-20 ☐	9:1-29 ☐	10:1-22 ☐	11:1-32 ☐	12:1-32 ☐	13:1—14:21 ☐

Reading Schedule for the Recovery Version of the Old Testament with Footnotes

Wk.	Lord's Day	Monday	Tuesday	Wednesday	Thursday	Friday	Saturday
27	14:22—15:23 ☐	16:1-22 ☐	17:1—18:8 ☐	18:9—19:21 ☐	20:1—21:17 ☐	21:18—22:30 ☐	23:1-25 ☐
28	24:1-22 ☐	25:1-19 ☐	26:1-19 ☐	27:1-26 ☐	28:1-68 ☐	29:1-29 ☐	30:1—31:29 ☐
29	31:30—32:52 ☐	33:1-29 ☐	34:1-12 ☐	Josh. 1:1-18 ☐	2:1-24 ☐	3:1-17 ☐	4:1-24 ☐
30	5:1-15 ☐	6:1-27 ☐	7:1-26 ☐	8:1-35 ☐	9:1-27 ☐	10:1-43 ☐	11:1—12:24 ☐
31	13:1-33 ☐	14:1—15:63 ☐	16:1—18:28 ☐	19:1-51 ☐	20:1—21:45 ☐	22:1-34 ☐	23:1—24:33 ☐
32	Judg. 1:1-36 ☐	2:1-23 ☐	3:1-31 ☐	4:1-24 ☐	5:1-31 ☐	6:1-40 ☐	7:1-25 ☐
33	8:1-35 ☐	9:1-57 ☐	10:1—11:40 ☐	12:1—13:25 ☐	14:1—15:20 ☐	16:1-31 ☐	17:1—18:31 ☐
34	19:1-30 ☐	20:1-48 ☐	21:1-25 ☐	Ruth 1:1-22 ☐	2:1-23 ☐	3:1-18 ☐	4:1-22 ☐
35	1 Sam. 1:1-28 ☐	2:1-36 ☐	3:1—4:22 ☐	5:1—6:21 ☐	7:1—8:22 ☐	9:1-27 ☐	10:1—11:15 ☐
36	12:1—13:23 ☐	14:1-52 ☐	15:1-35 ☐	16:1-23 ☐	17:1-58 ☐	18:1-30 ☐	19:1-24 ☐
37	20:1-42 ☐	21:1—22:23 ☐	23:1—24:22 ☐	25:1-44 ☐	26:1-25 ☐	27:1—28:25 ☐	29:1—30:31 ☐
38	31:1-13 ☐	2 Sam. 1:1-27 ☐	2:1-32 ☐	3:1-39 ☐	4:1—5:25 ☐	6:1-23 ☐	7:1-29 ☐
39	8:1—9:13 ☐	10:1—11:27 ☐	12:1-31 ☐	13:1-39 ☐	14:1-33 ☐	15:1—16:23 ☐	17:1—18:33 ☐
40	19:1-43 ☐	20:1—21:22 ☐	22:1-51 ☐	23:1-39 ☐	24:1-25 ☐	1 Kings 1:1-19 ☐	1:20-53 ☐
41	2:1-46 ☐	3:1-28 ☐	4:1-34 ☐	5:1—6:38 ☐	7:1-22 ☐	7:23-51 ☐	8:1-36 ☐
42	8:37-66 ☐	9:1-28 ☐	10:1-29 ☐	11:1-43 ☐	12:1-33 ☐	13:1-34 ☐	14:1-31 ☐
43	15:1-34 ☐	16:1—17:24 ☐	18:1-46 ☐	19:1-21 ☐	20:1-43 ☐	21:1—22:53 ☐	2 Kings 1:1-18 ☐
44	2:1—3:27 ☐	4:1-44 ☐	5:1—6:33 ☐	7:1-20 ☐	8:1-29 ☐	9:1-37 ☐	10:1-36 ☐
45	11:1—12:21 ☐	13:1—14:29 ☐	15:1-38 ☐	16:1-20 ☐	17:1-41 ☐	18:1-37 ☐	19:1-37 ☐
46	20:1—21:26 ☐	22:1-20 ☐	23:1-37 ☐	24:1—25:30 ☐	1 Chron. 1:1-54 ☐	2:1—3:24 ☐	4:1—5:26 ☐
47	6:1-81 ☐	7:1-40 ☐	8:1-40 ☐	9:1-44 ☐	10:1—11:47 ☐	12:1-40 ☐	13:1—14:17 ☐
48	15:1—16:43 ☐	17:1-27 ☐	18:1—19:19 ☐	20:1—21:30 ☐	22:1—23:32 ☐	24:1—25:31 ☐	26:1-32 ☐
49	27:1-34 ☐	28:1—29:30 ☐	2 Chron. 1:1-17 ☐	2:1—3:17 ☐	4:1—5:14 ☐	6:1-42 ☐	7:1—8:18 ☐
50	9:1—10:19 ☐	11:1—12:16 ☐	13:1—15:19 ☐	16:1—17:19 ☐	18:1—19:11 ☐	20:1-37 ☐	21:1—22:12 ☐
51	23:1—24:27 ☐	25:1—26:23 ☐	27:1—28:27 ☐	29:1-36 ☐	30:1—31:21 ☐	32:1-33 ☐	33:1—34:33 ☐
52	35:1—36:23 ☐	Ezra 1:1-11 ☐	2:1-70 ☐	3:1—4:24 ☐	5:1—6:22 ☐	7:1-28 ☐	8:1-36 ☐

Reading Schedule for the Recovery Version of the Old Testament with Footnotes

Wk.	Lord's Day	Monday	Tuesday	Wednesday	Thursday	Friday	Saturday
53	9:1—10:44 ☐	Neh. 1:1-11 ☐	2:1—3:32 ☐	4:1—5:19 ☐	6:1-19 ☐	7:1-73 ☐	8:1-18 ☐
54	9:1-20 ☐	9:21-38 ☐	10:1—11:36 ☐	12:1-47 ☐	13:1-31 ☐	Esth. 1:1-22 ☐	2:1—3:15 ☐
55	4:1—5:14 ☐	6:1—7:10 ☐	8:1-17 ☐	9:1—10:3 ☐	Job 1:1-22 ☐	2:1—3:26 ☐	4:1—5:27 ☐
56	6:1—7:21 ☐	8:1—9:35 ☐	10:1—11:20 ☐	12:1—13:28 ☐	14:1—15:35 ☐	16:1—17:16 ☐	18:1—19:29 ☐
57	20:1—21:34 ☐	22:1—23:17 ☐	24:1—25:6 ☐	26:1—27:23 ☐	28:1—29:25 ☐	30:1—31:40 ☐	32:1—33:33 ☐
58	34:1—35:16 ☐	36:1-33 ☐	37:1-24 ☐	38:1-41 ☐	39:1-30 ☐	40:1-24 ☐	41:1-34 ☐
59	42:1-17 ☐	Psa. 1:1-6 ☐	2:1—3:8 ☐	4:1—6:10 ☐	7:1—8:9 ☐	9:1—10:18 ☐	11:1—15:5 ☐
60	16:1—17:15 ☐	18:1-50 ☐	19:1—21:13 ☐	22:1-31 ☐	23:1—24:10 ☐	25:1—27:14 ☐	28:1—30:12 ☐
61	31:1—32:11 ☐	33:1—34:22 ☐	35:1—36:12 ☐	37:1-40 ☐	38:1—39:13 ☐	40:1—41:13 ☐	42:1—43:5 ☐
62	44:1-26 ☐	45:1-17 ☐	46:1—48:14 ☐	49:1—50:23 ☐	51:1—52:9 ☐	53:1—55:23 ☐	56:1—58:11 ☐
63	59:1—61:8 ☐	62:1—64:10 ☐	65:1—67:7 ☐	68:1-35 ☐	69:1—70:5 ☐	71:1—72:20 ☐	73:1—74:23 ☐
64	75:1—77:20 ☐	78:1-72 ☐	79:1—81:16 ☐	82:1—84:12 ☐	85:1—87:7 ☐	88:1—89:52 ☐	90:1—91:16 ☐
65	92:1—94:23 ☐	95:1—97:12 ☐	98:1—101:8 ☐	102:1—103:22 ☐	104:1—105:45 ☐	106:1-48 ☐	107:1-43 ☐
66	108:1—109:31 ☐	110:1—112:10 ☐	113:1—115:18 ☐	116:1—118:29 ☐	119:1-32 ☐	119:33-72 ☐	119:73-120 ☐
67	119:121-176 ☐	120:1—124:8 ☐	125:1—128:6 ☐	129:1—132:18 ☐	133:1—135:21 ☐	136:1—138:8 ☐	139:1—140:13 ☐
68	141:1—144:15 ☐	145:1—147:20 ☐	148:1—150:6 ☐	Prov. 1:1-33 ☐	2:1—3:35 ☐	4:1—5:23 ☐	6:1-35 ☐
69	7:1—8:36 ☐	9:1—10:32 ☐	11:1—12:28 ☐	13:1—14:35 ☐	15:1-33 ☐	16:1-33 ☐	17:1-28 ☐
70	18:1-24 ☐	19:1—20:30 ☐	21:1—22:29 ☐	23:1-35 ☐	24:1—25:28 ☐	26:1—27:27 ☐	28:1—29:27 ☐
71	30:1-33 ☐	31:1-31 ☐	Eccl. 1:1-18 ☐	2:1—3:22 ☐	4:1—5:20 ☐	6:1—7:29 ☐	8:1—9:18 ☐
72	10:1—11:10 ☐	12:1-14 ☐	S.S. 1:1-8 ☐	1:9-17 ☐	2:1-17 ☐	3:1-11 ☐	4:1-8 ☐
73	4:9-16 ☐	5:1-16 ☐	6:1-13 ☐	7:1-13 ☐	8:1-14 ☐	Isa. 1:1-11 ☐	1:12-31 ☐
74	2:1-22 ☐	3:1-26 ☐	4:1-6 ☐	5:1-30 ☐	6:1-13 ☐	7:1-25 ☐	8:1-22 ☐
75	9:1-21 ☐	10:1-34 ☐	11:1—12:6 ☐	13:1-22 ☐	14:1-14 ☐	14:15-32 ☐	15:1—16:14 ☐
76	17:1—18:7 ☐	19:1-25 ☐	20:1—21:17 ☐	22:1-25 ☐	23:1-18 ☐	24:1-23 ☐	25:1-12 ☐
77	26:1-21 ☐	27:1-13 ☐	28:1-29 ☐	29:1-24 ☐	30:1-33 ☐	31:1—32:20 ☐	33:1-24 ☐
78	34:1-17 ☐	35:1-10 ☐	36:1-22 ☐	37:1-38 ☐	38:1—39:8 ☐	40:1-31 ☐	41:1-29 ☐

Reading Schedule for the Recovery Version of the Old Testament with Footnotes

Wk.	Lord's Day	Monday	Tuesday	Wednesday	Thursday	Friday	Saturday
79	42:1-25 ☐	43:1-28 ☐	44:1-28 ☐	45:1-25 ☐	46:1-13 ☐	47:1-15 ☐	48:1-22 ☐
80	49:1-13 ☐	49:14-26 ☐	50:1—51:23 ☐	52:1-15 ☐	53:1-12 ☐	54:1-17 ☐	55:1-13 ☐
81	56:1-12 ☐	57:1-21 ☐	58:1-14 ☐	59:1-21 ☐	60:1-22 ☐	61:1-11 ☐	62:1-12 ☐
82	63:1-19 ☐	64:1-12 ☐	65:1-25 ☐	66:1-24 ☐	Jer. 1:1-19 ☐	2:1-19 ☐	2:20-37 ☐
83	3:1-25 ☐	4:1-31 ☐	5:1-31 ☐	6:1-30 ☐	7:1-34 ☐	8:1-22 ☐	9:1-26 ☐
84	10:1-25 ☐	11:1—12:17 ☐	13:1-27 ☐	14:1-22 ☐	15:1-21 ☐	16:1—17:27 ☐	18:1-23 ☐
85	19:1—20:18 ☐	21:1—22:30 ☐	23:1-40 ☐	24:1—25:38 ☐	26:1—27:22 ☐	28:1—29:32 ☐	30:1-24 ☐
86	31:1-23 ☐	31:24-40 ☐	32:1-44 ☐	33:1-26 ☐	34:1-22 ☐	35:1-19 ☐	36:1-32 ☐
87	37:1-21 ☐	38:1-28 ☐	39:1—40:16 ☐	41:1—42:22 ☐	43:1—44:30 ☐	45:1—46:28 ☐	47:1—48:16 ☐
88	48:17-47 ☐	49:1-22 ☐	49:23-39 ☐	50:1-27 ☐	50:28-46 ☐	51:1-27 ☐	51:28-64 ☐
89	52:1-34 ☐	Lam. 1:1-22 ☐	2:1-22 ☐	3:1-39 ☐	3:40-66 ☐	4:1-22 ☐	5:1-22 ☐
90	Ezek. 1:1-14 ☐	1:15-28 ☐	2:1—3:27 ☐	4:1—5:17 ☐	6:1—7:27 ☐	8:1—9:11 ☐	10:1—11:25 ☐
91	12:1—13:23 ☐	14:1—15:8 ☐	16:1-63 ☐	17:1—18:32 ☐	19:1-14 ☐	20:1-49 ☐	21:1-32 ☐
92	22:1-31 ☐	23:1-49 ☐	24:1-27 ☐	25:1—26:21 ☐	27:1-36 ☐	28:1-26 ☐	29:1—30:26 ☐
93	31:1—32:32 ☐	33:1-33 ☐	34:1-31 ☐	35:1—36:21 ☐	36:22-38 ☐	37:1-28 ☐	38:1—39:29 ☐
94	40:1-27 ☐	40:28-49 ☐	41:1-26 ☐	42:1—43:27 ☐	44:1-31 ☐	45:1-25 ☐	46:1-24 ☐
95	47:1-23 ☐	48:1-35 ☐	Dan. 1:1-21 ☐	2:1-30 ☐	2:31-49 ☐	3:1-30 ☐	4:1-37 ☐
96	5:1-31 ☐	6:1-28 ☐	7:1-12 ☐	7:13-28 ☐	8:1-27 ☐	9:1-27 ☐	10:1-21 ☐
97	11:1-22 ☐	11:23-45 ☐	12:1-13 ☐	Hosea 1:1-11 ☐	2:1-23 ☐	3:1—4:19 ☐	5:1-15 ☐
98	6:1-11 ☐	7:1-16 ☐	8:1-14 ☐	9:1-17 ☐	10:1-15 ☐	11:1-12 ☐	12:1-14 ☐
99	13:1—14:9 ☐	Joel 1:1-20 ☐	2:1-16 ☐	2:17-32 ☐	3:1-21 ☐	Amos 1:1-15 ☐	2:1-16 ☐
100	3:1-15 ☐	4:1—5:27 ☐	6:1—7:17 ☐	8:1—9:15 ☐	Obad. 1-21 ☐	Jonah 1:1-17 ☐	2:1—4:11 ☐
101	Micah 1:1-16 ☐	2:1—3:12 ☐	4:1—5:15 ☐	6:1—7:20 ☐	Nahum 1:1-15 ☐	2:1—3:19 ☐	Hab. 1:1-17 ☐
102	2:1-20 ☐	3:1-19 ☐	Zeph. 1:1-18 ☐	2:1-15 ☐	3:1-20 ☐	Hag. 1:1-15 ☐	2:1-23 ☐
103	Zech. 1:1-21 ☐	2:1-13 ☐	3:1-10 ☐	4:1-14 ☐	5:1—6:15 ☐	7:1—8:23 ☐	9:1-17 ☐
104	10:1—11:17 ☐	12:1—13:9 ☐	14:1-21 ☐	Mal. 1:1-14 ☐	2:1-17 ☐	3:1-18 ☐	4:1-6 ☐

Reading Schedule for the Recovery Version of the New Testament with Footnotes

Wk.	Lord's Day	Monday	Tuesday	Wednesday	Thursday	Friday	Saturday
1	Matt. 1:1-2 ☐	1:3-7 ☐	1:8-17 ☐	1:18-25 ☐	2:1-23 ☐	3:1-6 ☐	3:7-17 ☐
2	4:1-11 ☐	4:12-25 ☐	5:1-4 ☐	5:5-12 ☐	5:13-20 ☐	5:21-26 ☐	5:27-48 ☐
3	6:1-8 ☐	6:9-18 ☐	6:19-34 ☐	7:1-12 ☐	7:13-29 ☐	8:1-13 ☐	8:14-22 ☐
4	8:23-34 ☐	9:1-13 ☐	9:14-17 ☐	9:18-34 ☐	9:35—10:5 ☐	10:6-25 ☐	10:26-42 ☐
5	11:1-15 ☐	11:16-30 ☐	12:1-14 ☐	12:15-32 ☐	12:33-42 ☐	12:43—13:2 ☐	13:3-12 ☐
6	13:13-30 ☐	13:31-43 ☐	13:44-58 ☐	14:1-13 ☐	14:14-21 ☐	14:22-36 ☐	15:1-20 ☐
7	15:21-31 ☐	15:32-39 ☐	16:1-12 ☐	16:13-20 ☐	16:21-28 ☐	17:1-13 ☐	17:14-27 ☐
8	18:1-14 ☐	18:15-22 ☐	18:23-35 ☐	19:1-15 ☐	19:16-30 ☐	20:1-16 ☐	20:17-34 ☐
9	21:1-11 ☐	21:12-22 ☐	21:23-32 ☐	21:33-46 ☐	22:1-22 ☐	22:23-33 ☐	22:34-46 ☐
10	23:1-12 ☐	23:13-39 ☐	24:1-14 ☐	24:15-31 ☐	24:32-51 ☐	25:1-13 ☐	25:14-30 ☐
11	25:31-46 ☐	26:1-16 ☐	26:17-35 ☐	26:36-46 ☐	26:47-64 ☐	26:65-75 ☐	27:1-26 ☐
12	27:27-44 ☐	27:45-56 ☐	27:57—28:15 ☐	28:16-20 ☐	Mark 1:1 ☐	1:2-6 ☐	1:7-13 ☐
13	1:14-28 ☐	1:29-45 ☐	2:1-12 ☐	2:13-28 ☐	3:1-19 ☐	3:20-35 ☐	4:1-25 ☐
14	4:26-41 ☐	5:1-20 ☐	5:21-43 ☐	6:1-29 ☐	6:30-56 ☐	7:1-23 ☐	7:24-37 ☐
15	8:1-26 ☐	8:27—9:1 ☐	9:2-29 ☐	9:30-50 ☐	10:1-16 ☐	10:17-34 ☐	10:35-52 ☐
16	11:1-16 ☐	11:17-33 ☐	12:1-27 ☐	12:28-44 ☐	13:1-13 ☐	13:14-37 ☐	14:1-26 ☐
17	14:27-52 ☐	14:53-72 ☐	15:1-15 ☐	15:16-47 ☐	16:1-8 ☐	16:9-20 ☐	Luke 1:1-4 ☐
18	1:5-25 ☐	1:26-46 ☐	1:47-56 ☐	1:57-80 ☐	2:1-8 ☐	2:9-20 ☐	2:21-39 ☐
19	2:40-52 ☐	3:1-20 ☐	3:21-38 ☐	4:1-13 ☐	4:14-30 ☐	4:31-44 ☐	5:1-26 ☐
20	5:27—6:16 ☐	6:17-38 ☐	6:39-49 ☐	7:1-17 ☐	7:18-23 ☐	7:24-35 ☐	7:36-50 ☐
21	8:1-15 ☐	8:16-25 ☐	8:26-39 ☐	8:40-56 ☐	9:1-17 ☐	9:18-26 ☐	9:27-36 ☐
22	9:37-50 ☐	9:51-62 ☐	10:1-11 ☐	10:12-24 ☐	10:25-37 ☐	10:38-42 ☐	11:1-13 ☐
23	11:14-26 ☐	11:27-36 ☐	11:37-54 ☐	12:1-12 ☐	12:13-21 ☐	12:22-34 ☐	12:35-48 ☐
24	12:49-59 ☐	13:1-9 ☐	13:10-17 ☐	13:18-30 ☐	13:31—14:6 ☐	14:7-14 ☐	14:15-24 ☐
25	14:25-35 ☐	15:1-10 ☐	15:11-21 ☐	15:22-32 ☐	16:1-13 ☐	16:14-22 ☐	16:23-31 ☐
26	17:1-19 ☐	17:20-37 ☐	18:1-14 ☐	18:15-30 ☐	18:31-43 ☐	19:1-10 ☐	19:11-27 ☐

Reading Schedule for the Recovery Version of the New Testament with Footnotes

Wk.	Lord's Day	Monday	Tuesday	Wednesday	Thursday	Friday	Saturday
27	Luke 19:28-48 ☐	20:1-19 ☐	20:20-38 ☐	20:39—21:4 ☐	21:5-27 ☐	21:28-38 ☐	22:1-20 ☐
28	22:21-38 ☐	22:39-54 ☐	22:55-71 ☐	23:1-43 ☐	23:44-56 ☐	24:1-12 ☐	24:13-35 ☐
29	24:36-53 ☐	John 1:1-13 ☐	1:14-18 ☐	1:19-34 ☐	1:35-51 ☐	2:1-11 ☐	2:12-22 ☐
30	2:23—3:13 ☐	3:14-21 ☐	3:22-36 ☐	4:1-14 ☐	4:15-26 ☐	4:27-42 ☐	4:43-54 ☐
31	5:1-16 ☐	5:17-30 ☐	5:31-47 ☐	6:1-15 ☐	6:16-31 ☐	6:32-51 ☐	6:52-71 ☐
32	7:1-9 ☐	7:10-24 ☐	7:25-36 ☐	7:37-52 ☐	7:53—8:11 ☐	8:12-27 ☐	8:28-44 ☐
33	8:45-59 ☐	9:1-13 ☐	9:14-34 ☐	9:35—10:9 ☐	10:10-30 ☐	10:31—11:4 ☐	11:5-22 ☐
34	11:23-40 ☐	11:41-57 ☐	12:1-11 ☐	12:12-24 ☐	12:25-36 ☐	12:37-50 ☐	13:1-11 ☐
35	13:12-30 ☐	13:31-38 ☐	14:1-6 ☐	14:7-20 ☐	14:21-31 ☐	15:1-11 ☐	15:12-27 ☐
36	16:1-15 ☐	16:16-33 ☐	17:1-5 ☐	17:6-13 ☐	17:14-24 ☐	17:25—18:11 ☐	18:12-27 ☐
37	18:28-40 ☐	19:1-16 ☐	19:17-30 ☐	19:31-42 ☐	20:1-13 ☐	20:14-18 ☐	20:19-22 ☐
38	20:23-31 ☐	21:1-14 ☐	21:15-22 ☐	21:23-25 ☐	Acts 1:1-8 ☐	1:9-14 ☐	1:15-26 ☐
39	2:1-13 ☐	2:14-21 ☐	2:22-36 ☐	2:37-41 ☐	2:42-47 ☐	3:1-18 ☐	3:19—4:22 ☐
40	4:23-37 ☐	5:1-16 ☐	5:17-32 ☐	5:33-42 ☐	6:1—7:1 ☐	7:2-29 ☐	7:30-60 ☐
41	8:1-13 ☐	8:14-25 ☐	8:26-40 ☐	9:1-19 ☐	9:20-43 ☐	10:1-16 ☐	10:17-33 ☐
42	10:34-48 ☐	11:1-18 ☐	11:19-30 ☐	12:1-25 ☐	13:1-12 ☐	13:13-43 ☐	13:44—14:5 ☐
43	14:6-28 ☐	15:1-12 ☐	15:13-34 ☐	15:35—16:5 ☐	16:6-18 ☐	16:19-40 ☐	17:1-18 ☐
44	17:19-34 ☐	18:1-17 ☐	18:18-28 ☐	19:1-20 ☐	19:21-41 ☐	20:1-12 ☐	20:13-38 ☐
45	21:1-14 ☐	21:15-26 ☐	21:27-40 ☐	22:1-21 ☐	22:22-29 ☐	22:30—23:11 ☐	23:12-15 ☐
46	23:16-30 ☐	23:31—24:21 ☐	24:22—25:5 ☐	25:6-27 ☐	26:1-13 ☐	26:14-32 ☐	27:1-26 ☐
47	27:27—28:10 ☐	28:11-22 ☐	28:23-31 ☐	Rom. 1:1-2 ☐	1:3-7 ☐	1:8-17 ☐	1:18-25 ☐
48	1:26—2:10 ☐	2:11-29 ☐	3:1-20 ☐	3:21-31 ☐	4:1-12 ☐	4:13-25 ☐	5:1-11 ☐
49	5:12-17 ☐	5:18—6:5 ☐	6:6-11 ☐	6:12-23 ☐	7:1-12 ☐	7:13-25 ☐	8:1-2 ☐
50	8:3-6 ☐	8:7-13 ☐	8:14-25 ☐	8:26-39 ☐	9:1-18 ☐	9:19—10:3 ☐	10:4-15 ☐
51	10:16—11:10 ☐	11:11-22 ☐	11:23-36 ☐	12:1-3 ☐	12:4-21 ☐	13:1-14 ☐	14:1-12 ☐
52	14:13-23 ☐	15:1-13 ☐	15:14-33 ☐	16:1-5 ☐	16:6-24 ☐	16:25-27 ☐	1 Cor. 1:1-4 ☐

Reading Schedule for the Recovery Version of the New Testament with Footnotes

Wk.	Lord's Day	Monday	Tuesday	Wednesday	Thursday	Friday	Saturday
53	☐ 1 Cor. 1:5-9	☐ 1:10-17	☐ 1:18-31	☐ 2:1-5	☐ 2:6-10	☐ 2:11-16	☐ 3:1-9
54	☐ 3:10-13	☐ 3:14-23	☐ 4:1-9	☐ 4:10-21	☐ 5:1-13	☐ 6:1-11	☐ 6:12-20
55	☐ 7:1-16	☐ 7:17-24	☐ 7:25-40	☐ 8:1-13	☐ 9:1-15	☐ 9:16-27	☐ 10:1-4
56	☐ 10:5-13	☐ 10:14-33	☐ 11:1-6	☐ 11:7-16	☐ 11:17-26	☐ 11:27-34	☐ 12:1-11
57	☐ 12:12-22	☐ 12:23-31	☐ 13:1-13	☐ 14:1-12	☐ 14:13-25	☐ 14:26-33	☐ 14:34-40
58	☐ 15:1-19	☐ 15:20-28	☐ 15:29-34	☐ 15:35-49	☐ 15:50-58	☐ 16:1-9	☐ 16:10-24
59	☐ 2 Cor. 1:1-4	☐ 1:5-14	☐ 1:15-22	☐ 1:23—2:11	☐ 2:12-17	☐ 3:1-6	☐ 3:7-11
60	☐ 3:12-18	☐ 4:1-6	☐ 4:7-12	☐ 4:13-18	☐ 5:1-8	☐ 5:9-15	☐ 5:16-21
61	☐ 6:1-13	☐ 6:14—7:4	☐ 7:5-16	☐ 8:1-15	☐ 8:16-24	☐ 9:1-15	☐ 10:1-6
62	☐ 10:7-18	☐ 11:1-15	☐ 11:16-33	☐ 12:1-10	☐ 12:11-21	☐ 13:1-10	☐ 13:11-14
63	☐ Gal. 1:1-5	☐ 1:6-14	☐ 1:15-24	☐ 2:1-13	☐ 2:14-21	☐ 3:1-4	☐ 3:5-14
64	☐ 3:15-22	☐ 3:23-29	☐ 4:1-7	☐ 4:8-20	☐ 4:21-31	☐ 5:1-12	☐ 5:13-21
65	☐ 5:22-26	☐ 6:1-10	☐ 6:11-15	☐ 6:16-18	☐ Eph. 1:1-3	☐ 1:4-6	☐ 1:7-10
66	☐ 1:11-14	☐ 1:15-18	☐ 1:19-23	☐ 2:1-5	☐ 2:6-10	☐ 2:11-14	☐ 2:15-18
67	☐ 2:19-22	☐ 3:1-7	☐ 3:8-13	☐ 3:14-18	☐ 3:19-21	☐ 4:1-4	☐ 4:5-10
68	☐ 4:11-16	☐ 4:17-24	☐ 4:25-32	☐ 5:1-10	☐ 5:11-21	☐ 5:22-26	☐ 5:27-33
69	☐ 6:1-9	☐ 6:10-14	☐ 6:15-18	☐ 6:19-24	☐ Phil. 1:1-7	☐ 1:8-18	☐ 1:19-26
70	☐ 1:27—2:4	☐ 2:5-11	☐ 2:12-16	☐ 2:17-30	☐ 3:1-6	☐ 3:7-11	☐ 3:12-16
71	☐ 3:17-21	☐ 4:1-9	☐ 4:10-23	☐ Col. 1:1-8	☐ 1:9-13	☐ 1:14-23	☐ 1:24-29
72	☐ 2:1-7	☐ 2:8-15	☐ 2:16-23	☐ 3:1-4	☐ 3:5-15	☐ 3:16-25	☐ 4:1-18
73	☐ 1 Thes. 1:1-3	☐ 1:4-10	☐ 2:1-12	☐ 2:13—3:5	☐ 3:6-13	☐ 4:1-10	☐ 4:11—5:11
74	☐ 5:12-28	☐ 2 Thes. 1:1-12	☐ 2:1-17	☐ 3:1-18	☐ 1 Tim. 1:1-2	☐ 1:3-4	☐ 1:5-14
75	☐ 1:15-20	☐ 2:1-7	☐ 2:8-15	☐ 3:1-13	☐ 3:14—4:5	☐ 4:6-16	☐ 5:1-25
76	☐ 6:1-10	☐ 6:11-21	☐ 2 Tim. 1:1-10	☐ 1:11-18	☐ 2:1-15	☐ 2:16-26	☐ 3:1-13
77	☐ 3:14—4:8	☐ 4:9-22	☐ Titus 1:1-4	☐ 1:5-16	☐ 2:1-15	☐ 3:1-8	☐ 3:9-15
78	☐ Philem. 1:1-11	☐ 1:12-25	☐ Heb. 1:1-2	☐ 1:3-5	☐ 1:6-14	☐ 2:1-9	☐ 2:10-18

Reading Schedule for the Recovery Version of the New Testament with Footnotes

Wk.	Lord's Day	Monday	Tuesday	Wednesday	Thursday	Friday	Saturday
79	Heb. 3:1-6 ☐	3:7-19 ☐	4:1-9 ☐	4:10-13 ☐	4:14-16 ☐	5:1-10 ☐	5:11—6:3 ☐
80	6:4-8 ☐	6:9-20 ☐	7:1-10 ☐	7:11-28 ☐	8:1-6 ☐	8:7-13 ☐	9:1-4 ☐
81	9:5-14 ☐	9:15-28 ☐	10:1-18 ☐	10:19-28 ☐	10:29-39 ☐	11:1-6 ☐	11:7-19 ☐
82	11:20-31 ☐	11:32-40 ☐	12:1-2 ☐	12:3-13 ☐	12:14-17 ☐	12:18-26 ☐	12:27-29 ☐
83	13:1-7 ☐	13:8-12 ☐	13:13-15 ☐	13:16-25 ☐	James 1:1-8 ☐	1:9-18 ☐	1:19-27 ☐
84	2:1-13 ☐	2:14-26 ☐	3:1-18 ☐	4:1-10 ☐	4:11-17 ☐	5:1-12 ☐	5:13-20 ☐
85	1 Pet. 1:1-2 ☐	1:3-4 ☐	1:5 ☐	1:6-9 ☐	1:10-12 ☐	1:13-17 ☐	1:18-25 ☐
86	2:1-3 ☐	2:4-8 ☐	2:9-17 ☐	2:18-25 ☐	3:1-13 ☐	3:14-22 ☐	4:1-6 ☐
87	4:7-16 ☐	4:17-19 ☐	5:1-4 ☐	5:5-9 ☐	5:10-14 ☐	2 Pet. 1:1-2 ☐	1:3-4 ☐
88	1:5-8 ☐	1:9-11 ☐	1:12-18 ☐	1:19-21 ☐	2:1-3 ☐	2:4-11 ☐	2:12-22 ☐
89	3:1-6 ☐	3:7-9 ☐	3:10-12 ☐	3:13-15 ☐	3:16 ☐	3:17-18 ☐	1 John 1:1-2 ☐
90	1:3-4 ☐	1:5 ☐	1:6 ☐	1:7 ☐	1:8-10 ☐	2:1-2 ☐	2:3-11 ☐
91	2:12-14 ☐	2:15-19 ☐	2:20-23 ☐	2:24-27 ☐	2:28-29 ☐	3:1-5 ☐	3:6-10 ☐
92	3:11-18 ☐	3:19-24 ☐	4:1-6 ☐	4:7-11 ☐	4:12-15 ☐	4:16—5:3 ☐	5:4-13 ☐
93	5:14-17 ☐	5:18-21 ☐	2 John 1:1-3 ☐	1:4-9 ☐	1:10-13 ☐	3 John 1:1-6 ☐	1:7-14 ☐
94	Jude 1:-4 ☐	1:5-10 ☐	1:11-19 ☐	1:20-25 ☐	Rev. 1:1-3 ☐	1:4-6 ☐	1:7-11 ☐
95	1:12-13 ☐	1:14-16 ☐	1:17-20 ☐	2:1-6 ☐	2:7 ☐	2:8-9 ☐	2:10-11 ☐
96	2:12-14 ☐	2:15-17 ☐	2:18-23 ☐	2:24-29 ☐	3:1-3 ☐	3:4-6 ☐	3:7-9 ☐
97	3:10-13 ☐	3:14-18 ☐	3:19-22 ☐	4:1-5 ☐	4:6-7 ☐	4:8-11 ☐	5:1-6 ☐
98	5:7-14 ☐	6:1-8 ☐	6:9-17 ☐	7:1-8 ☐	7:9-17 ☐	8:1-6 ☐	8:7-12 ☐
99	8:13—9:11 ☐	9:12-21 ☐	10:1-4 ☐	10:5-11 ☐	11:1-4 ☐	11:5-14 ☐	11:15-19 ☐
100	12:1-4 ☐	12:5-9 ☐	12:10-18 ☐	13:1-10 ☐	13:11-18 ☐	14:1-5 ☐	14:6-12 ☐
101	14:13-20 ☐	15:1-8 ☐	16:1-12 ☐	16:13-21 ☐	17:1-6 ☐	17:7-18 ☐	18:1-8 ☐
102	18:9—19:4 ☐	19:5-10 ☐	19:11-16 ☐	19:17-21 ☐	20:1-6 ☐	20:7-10 ☐	20:11-15 ☐
103	21:1 ☐	21:2 ☐	21:3-8 ☐	21:9-13 ☐	21:14-18 ☐	21:19-21 ☐	21:22-27 ☐
104	22:1 ☐	22:2 ☐	22:3-11 ☐	22:12-15 ☐	22:16-17 ☐	22:18-21 ☐	

Week 1 — Day 4   **Today's verses**

Acts 2:45 And they sold their properties and possessions and divided them to all, as anyone had need.

2 Cor. 8:15 As it is written, "He who *gathered* much had no excess, and he who *gathered* little had no lack."

Date

Week 1 — Day 1   **Today's verses**

1 Thes. 1:9 For they themselves report concerning us what kind of entrance we had toward you and how you turned to God from the idols to serve a living and true God.

Matt. 5:3 Blessed are the poor in spirit, for theirs is the kingdom of the heavens.

Date

Week 1 — Day 5   **Today's verses**

Exo. 12:36 And the LORD gave the people favor in the sight of the Egyptians, so that they lent unto them *such things as they required:* and they spoiled the Egyptians.

Col. 3:5 Put to death therefore your members which are on the earth:...greediness, which is idolatry.

Date

Week 1 — Day 2   **Today's verses**

Luke 18:24b How difficult it is for those who have riches to go into the kingdom of God.

25 For it is easier for a camel to enter through the eye of a needle than for a rich man to enter into the kingdom of God.

Date

Week 1 — Day 6   **Today's verses**

Matt. 22:21b Then He said to them, Render then the things that are Caesar's to Caesar and the things that are God's to God.

1 Tim. 6:10 For the love of money is a root of all evils, *because of* which some, aspiring after money, have been led away from the faith and pierced themselves through with many pains.

Date

Week 1 — Day 3   **Today's verses**

Luke 19:8 And Zaccheus stood and said to the Lord, Behold, the half of my possessions, Lord, I give to the poor, and if I have taken anything from anyone by false accusation, I restore four times as much.

Phil. 4:15, 17 And you yourselves also know, Philippians, that in the beginning of the gospel, when I went out from Macedonia, no church had fellowship with me in the account of giving and receiving except you only....Not that I seek the gift, but I seek the fruit which increases to your account.

Date

Week 2 — Day 1 Today's verses

Matt. No one can serve two masters, for either
6:24 he will hate the one and love the other, or
he will hold to one and despise the other.
You cannot serve God and mammon.

_____
Date

Week 2 — Day 2 Today's verses

Matt. For where your treasure is, there will your
6:21 heart be also.
31-33 Therefore do not be anxious, saying,
What shall we eat? or, What shall we
drink? or, With what shall we be clothed?
For all these things the Gentiles are anxiously seeking. For your heavenly Father
knows that you need all these things. But
seek first His kingdom and His righteousness, and all these things will be added to
you.

_____
Date

Week 2 — Day 3 Today's verses

1 Cor. Now concerning the collection for the
16:1-2 saints, just as I directed the churches of
Galatia, so you also do. On the first day of
the week each one of you should lay
aside in store to himself whatever he may
have been prospered, that no collections
be made when I come.
Luke 6:38 Give, and it will be given to you; a good
measure, pressed down, shaken together,
and running over, they will give into your
bosom. For with what measure you measure, it shall be measured to you in return.

_____
Date

Week 2 — Day 4 Today's verses

Acts In all things I have shown you by example
20:35 that toiling in this way we ought to support the weak and to remember the words
of the Lord Jesus, that He Himself said, It
is more blessed to give than to receive.

_____
Date

Week 2 — Day 5 Today's verses

Phil. Not that I seek the gift, but I seek the fruit
4:17-19 which increases to your account. But I
have received in full all things and
abound; I have been filled, receiving from
Epaphroditus the things from you, a
sweet-smelling savor, an acceptable sacrifice, well-pleasing to God. And my God
will fill your every need according to His
riches, in glory, in Christ Jesus.

_____
Date

Week 2 — Day 6 Today's verses

Matt. But take care not to do your righteousness
6:1-4 before men in order to be gazed at by
them; otherwise, you have no reward
with your Father who is in the heavens.
Therefore when you give alms, do not
sound a trumpet before you as the hypocrites do in the synagogues and in the
streets, so that they may be glorified by
men. Truly I say to you, They have their
reward in full. But you, when you give
alms, do not let your left hand know what
your right hand is doing, so that your
alms may be in secret; and your Father
who sees in secret will repay you.

_____
Date

Week 3 — Day 4 Today's verses

Rom. 12:1-2 I exhort you therefore, brothers, through the compassions of God to present your bodies a living sacrifice, holy, well pleasing to God, which is your reasonable service. And do not be fashioned according to this age, but be transformed by the renewing of the mind that you may prove what the will of God is, that which is good and well pleasing and perfect.

Date

Week 3 — Day 5 Today's verses

Rom. 14:7-9 For none of us lives to himself, and none dies to himself; for whether we live, we live to the Lord, and whether we die, we die to the Lord. Therefore whether we live or we die, we are the Lord's. For Christ died and lived again for this, that He might be Lord both of the dead and of the living.

Date

Week 3 — Day 6 Today's verses

2 Cor. 5:15 And He died for all that those who live may no longer live to themselves but to Him who died for them and has been raised.

Matt. 24:45 Who then is the faithful and prudent slave, whom the master has set over his household to give them food at the proper time?

46 Blessed is that slave whom his master, when he comes, will find so doing.

Date

Week 3 — Day 1 Today's verses

Phil. 4:18 But I have received in full all things and abound; I have been filled, receiving from Epaphroditus the things from you, a sweet-smelling savor, an acceptable sacrifice, well-pleasing to God.

Date

Week 3 — Day 2 Today's verses

2 Cor. 5:13 For whether we were beside ourselves, it was to God; or whether we are sober-minded, it is for you.

Date

Week 3 — Day 3 Today's verses

Mal. 3:10 Bring the whole tithe to the storehouse that there may be food in My house; and prove Me, if you will, by this, says Jehovah of hosts, whether I will open to you the windows of heaven and pour out blessing for you until there is no room for it.

Heb. 13:15 Through Him then let us offer up a sacrifice of praise continually to God, that is, the fruit of lips confessing His name.

16 But do not forget doing good and sharing with others, for with such sacrifices God is well pleased.

Date

Week 4 — Day 6 Today's verses

1 Cor. On the first day of the week each one of
16:2 you should lay aside in store to himself
whatever he may have been prospered,
that no collections be made when I come.

_____
Date

Week 4 — Day 3 Today's verses

2 Cor. But *it is* out of equality; at the present time
8:14 your abundance for their lack that their
abundance also may be for your lack, so
that there may be equality;
15 As it is written, "He who *gathered* much
had no excess, and he who *gathered* little
had no lack."

_____
Date

Week 4 — Day 5 Today's verses

Phil. And you yourselves also know, Philip-
4:15-16 pians, that in the beginning of the gospel,
when I went out from Macedonia, no
church had fellowship with me in the account of giving and receiving except you
only; for even in Thessalonica you sent
both once and again to my need.
19 And my God will fill your every need according to His riches, in glory, in Christ
Jesus.

_____
Date

Week 4 — Day 2 Today's verses

2 Cor. As made sorrowful yet always rejoicing;
6:10 as poor yet enriching many; as having
nothing and yet possessing all things.
Phil. 4:12 I know also how to be abased, and I know
how to abound; in everything and in all
things I have learned the secret both to be
filled and to hunger, both to abound and
to lack.

_____
Date

Week 4 — Day 4 Today's verses

Acts 2:44 And all those who believed were together
and had all things common.
4:32 And the heart and soul of the multitude of
those who had believed was one; and not
even one said that any of his possessions
was his own, but all things were common
to them.

_____
Date

Week 4 — Day 1 Today's verses

Isa. 6:8 Then I heard the voice of the Lord, saying,
Whom shall I send? Who will go for us?
And I said, Here am I; send me.
Dan. The people who know their God will
11:32b show strength and take action.

_____
Date

Week 5 — Day 4   Today's verses

Matt. Do not store up for yourselves treasures
6:19-21 on the earth, where moth and rust consume and where thieves dig through and
steal. But store up for yourselves treasures
in heaven, where neither moth nor rust
consumes and where thieves do not dig
through nor steal. For where your treasure
is, there will your heart be also.
31-33 Therefore do not be anxious, saying, What
shall we eat? or, What shall we drink? or,
With what shall we be clothed? For all
these things the Gentiles are anxiously
seeking. For your heavenly Father knows
that you need all these things. But seek first
His kingdom and His righteousness, and all
these things will be added to you.

Date _____

Week 5 — Day 5   Today's verses

1 Tim. Charge those who are rich in the present
6:17-19 age not to be high-minded, nor to set their
hope on the uncertainty of riches but on
God, who affords us all things richly for
our enjoyment; to do good, to be rich in
good works, to be ready to distribute, to
be ones willing to share; laying away for
themselves a good foundation as a treasure for the future, that they may lay hold
on that which is really life.

Date _____

Week 5 — Day 6   Today's verses

1 Cor. Now concerning the collection for the
16:1-2 saints, just as I directed the churches of
Galatia, so you also do. On the first day of
the week each one of you should lay
aside in store to himself whatever he may
have been prospered, that no collections
be made when I come.

Date _____

Week 5 — Day 1   Today's verses

2 Cor. 8:7 But just as you abound in everything, in
faith and in word and in knowledge and
in all earnestness and in the love in you
from us, abound in this grace also.
13-15 For it is not that to others there would be
relief, yet to you affliction, but it is out of
equality; at the present time your abundance for their lack that their abundance
also may be for your lack, so that there
may be equality; as it is written, "He who
gathered much had no excess, and he
who gathered little had no lack."

Date _____

Week 5 — Day 2   Today's verses

2 Cor. But take note of this: He who sows spar-
9:6-7 ingly shall also sparingly reap; and he
who sows with blessings shall also with
blessings reap; each one as he has purposed in his heart, not out of sorrow or out
of necessity, for God loves a cheerful
giver.
Prov. There is one who scatters and increases
11:24 yet more, / And there is one who withholds what is appropriate, but ends up
only in want.

Date _____

Week 5 — Day 3   Today's verses

2 Cor. Now He who bountifully supplies seed to
9:10-11 the sower and bread for food will supply
and multiply your seed and cause the
fruits of your righteousness to increase.
You in everything are being enriched unto
all liberality, which works out through us
thanksgiving to God.

Date _____